Beyond Fear

Praise for Beyond Fear: A Woman's Path to Enlightenment

"This memoir of experiences on the road to enlightenment begins with the bang of life-altering confrontation and doesn't let up.

Readers who are intrigued by the possibilities of cultivating their own routes to enlightenment will follow in her footsteps as Chrappa tackles not just mountaineering, but matters of her own heart and growth… Chrappa captures thought-provoking growth experiences in a manner that will encourage readers to consider their own paths to growth.

While those expecting a boilerplate step-by-step plan might be surprised, the real value in *Beyond Fear: A Woman's Path to Enlightenment* lies in its ability to meld memoir with movement in a way readers can more easily absorb."

— *Midwest Book Review*

"An intimate memoir laced with ancient wisdom and contemporary insight, *Beyond Fear: A Woman's Path to Enlightenment* by Karen Chrappa is the story of our human journey through uncertainty into a realm of higher knowledge. From the author's traumatic childhood confessions and life-or-death experiences on mountainsides to overcoming addiction and the transformative power of psychotherapy and yoga, this book winds naturally from one vulnerable revelation and achievement to the next. Conversational yet profound discussions of religion, sexuality, femininity, spirituality, privacy, and motherhood give this empowering book a wide reach, while the author's raw storytelling power is immediately captivating from the first page."

— *Self Publishing Review*

"…Chrappa invites readers on a powerful journey of human resilience and discovery. With unflinching honesty, she shares her life's raw experiences and a determination to overcome. Chrappa emerges with profound understanding, an unwavering spirit, and radiates as a source of light and love. Along the way, she shares precious nuggets of wisdom, inspiring her readers to navigate life with greater clarity and purpose."

— Carolyn Calfee, author of *Discover Abiquiu from A to Z*

"Through rich storytelling and thoughtful contemplation, *Beyond Fear* is a book that reads like a river: strong, deep and ever-changing in its scope. Chrappa's story expresses the pain of divorce, death, unrequited love and loss, paired with her inconsolable longing for transformation. At the end of each chapter, she compels us to explore our life experiences through writing exercises, meditations, and ritual-making. We turn inward along with her, and learn how to navigate loss when our own lives are upended. Ultimately, this is a love story, a story of survival, compassion and strength and how the recognition of faith as surrender has the power to heal."

— Monica Devine, author of *Water Mask*

"Karen's profound journey of transformation reads like butter on hot toast. It is written with sweeping grace and honesty. I recommend it to anyone seeking inspiration, authentic spirituality or genuine feminine wisdom!"

— Marcela Lobos, author of *Awakening Your Inner Shaman*

"Karen Chrappa's *Beyond Fear: A Woman's Path to Enlightenment* is *Eat, Pray, Love* meets *Practicing Mindfulness*. A sensual and thoughtful memoir about love and self-realization, *Beyond Fear* sensitively tells the story of incredible heartache and the beauty that results from spiritual enlightenment. Moving, inspirational, and well-written!"

— Dawn Reno Langly, author of *The Mourning Parade*

KAREN CHRAPPA

BEYOND FEAR

A Woman's Path to Enlightenment

A MEMOIR

Mango Moon Media | New Mexico

Published by Terra Nova Books, an imprint of
Mango Moon Media, www.mangomoonmedia.com

The names and identifying characteristics of some people described in this book have been changed to protect privacy.

Printed in the United States of America

ISBN 978-1-948749-94-7
Library of Congress Control Number 2024917053

ACKNOWLEDGMENTS

My deepest gratitude extends to the lineage of women in my life whose hearts and mine are eternally linked. Thank you to my grandmothers, Lillian and Evelyn; thank you to my mother, Barbara; my sisters, Kristine and Michele; my aunts, Lilyan and Eileen; my nieces, Kailey and Shannon; and my daughters, Sarabeth and Danielle, who offered boundless support and encouragement through the many years of bringing this book to fruition.

I bow in gratitude to my father and grandfathers; to Phil, the father of my daughters, and grandfather to my granddaughter, Philippa, who watch over us from the other side. Thank you to my brothers, Stephen and Jason and my son in law, Mike, for being men of integrity in the world.

The book you are about to read would never have been possible without the visionary guidance of editor Tania Casselle. She saw seeds of potential in a fragile manuscript which blossomed through her skillful perceptions.

My deepest thanks for the support from the stellar team at Mango Moon who believed in a manuscript still in gestation. Thank you to Marty Gerber for his impeccable editing in shaping *Beyond Fear* to its highest potential. And to Janet Angulo for her superior cover design. A deep bow of gratitude to Mari Angulo and Lisa Madison for their commitment to bringing the voices of women to the world.

And finally, I am deeply grateful to our Earth Mother, Pachamama, for opening my eyes to your beauty and wonder. Thank you for transforming me with your healing, your compassion, and your immeasurable love.

CONTENTS

CHAPTER ONE

An Unintended Vision Quest

I KNOW I BROKE EVERY safety rule that fateful Sunday morning in November. I innocently set out to go hiking with Jethro, my scrappy tan and white terrier mix rescued a year earlier. There was no destination in mind other than heading north on the highway. I didn't expect to be gone long, and had left without food or water wearing a lightweight nylon jacket and moccasins. The decision to hike seemed so mundane it never occurred to me to let anyone know I was going.

It was an unusually warm November day in New Mexico with a cloudless turquoise sky. Jethro was always up for an adventure and nimbly jumped onto the front seat of my silver Hyundai Elantra as we headed north on U.S. Highway 84, which goes through the state from Texas to Colorado.

After a lifetime of living in New York, I had moved to New Mexico three years earlier. I'd spent the first two years living in Truth or Consequences, a quirky resort town about two hours north of the southern border. I had recently settled in Abiquiu, another remote town with a peculiar name which had been made famous by the artist Georgia O'Keeffe who lived and worked there.

Driving north, I was wondering where to stop and hike when I spotted a sign pointing to the Rim Vista trailhead. I had read about the Rim Vista in numerous guidebooks boasting some of the best views in the state. I took my happening to see the words Rim Vista as the perfect sign that this was the day to hike the New Mexico gem.

After parking at the trailhead, Jethro and I began our climb along a well-marked path cutting through rugged terrain. We hiked along the rim of rugged cliffs that offered one spectacular vista after another overlooking the red rock landscape that had inspired O'Keeffe. An hour or so later, at nearly 8,000 feet, I received a text that most likely saved my life.

"Can't find my peanut butter cups. Did you take both of them?" It was my friend Jon.

"No, I don't know where the peanut butter cups are," I texted back. "I'm out hiking the Rim Vista Trail."

Now, thanks to the missing peanut butter cups, someone knew where I was. By the time Jon and I finished texting, my phone was nearly dead. I hadn't thought to take the time to charge it before leaving for the day. Jon's last words to me were, "Keep your feet on the ground."

"Okay," I answered and shut down my phone to conserve any energy that was left.

Although the hike up seemed clear, the path going down did not. As I walked along the cliffs, I wondered if I was on the trail or not. I hiked back to the last visible marker I could find: a pink plastic ribbon hanging from a juniper branch. Then back and forth, over and over, I walked until I no longer had a clue as to what was the trail and what was not.

By now, the only thought in my mind was: *I have to get down.* It had been early afternoon when we first hit the trail, later than usual to start out on a hike. Sunlight was waning. The clocks had been turned back the night before to end daylight savings time. Light would be lost an hour earlier. Maneuvering through the rough terrain was tough enough during the day; going down without light would be impossible.

An ancient avalanche of rocks had wedged itself into the earth, making an arduous descent for Jethro and me. Sometimes, the jagged contours were more than he wanted to traverse, and he retreated back up. I made a makeshift leash from the sleeve of my nylon jacket which I tied around his collar, and we continued on down. When we seemed to be at a stretch of craggy terrain that Jethro couldn't manage on his own, I carried him.

The rock-filled chute opened to a cavernous arroyo, a dry river bed deep as a canyon. There was nothing to do but head back up. We kept hiking along the mountainside looking for a path that would lead us to the trailhead. Each thread of a trail hit a dead end that left us nowhere to go but back up again.

One rocky descent eventually flattened out at a smooth, sloped ledge. The only way to go lower was to slide along the limestone ridge. With no other thought than getting down, I sat on my bottom, leaned back, and slid along the ledge, hoping that Jethro would follow. At the bottom, I fell hard off a ledge jutting out two feet to the flat ground six feet below.

Standing on tiptoes to see over the limestone ledge, I found Jethro sitting still as stone about a hundred feet away. His ears stood straight up, stiff at attention, my black nylon jacket still tied around his collar.

I called to him but he wouldn't budge, not even an inch. I looked everywhere for a way back over the ledge to reach him but none of the nearby rocks could give me enough height or leverage to climb back up. The last light of day was ready to drop below the horizon. There was nowhere else to go, nothing else I could do.

I have had other dogs in my life, throughout both my childhood and while my children were young, but Jethro was the first one to truly feel like a companion. He was my family. He loved so generously and unconditionally. The map at the entrance to the trail had warned of bears and mountain lions. Jethro stood no chance. If anything happened to him that night, it would have been because I put him in peril. I don't know how I could have lived with myself after that.

I surrendered to the thought that where I had landed was where I would be spending the night. There was no way I would keep trying to get down the mountain and leave Jethro behind. I felt suspended in a state of disbelief. Part of me thought this could not actually be happening, yet the gravity of the situation slapped me into a reality that left me wondering how I would survive. I looked around and thought about what I might need to get through the night. I was woefully unprepared.

I had never imagined that my innocent impulse to hike with my dog would leave me alone on the side of a mountain in a remote wilderness, with no one knowing where I was. I couldn't see Jethro from under the ledge but he was close enough to hear his painful high-pitched whimpers.

I have no wilderness experience. I could count on one hand the number of times I've been camping. Although I love nature and the outdoors, I was in a situation far beyond anything I had ever experienced. I don't even know how to use a compass, nor would it have made a difference if I had one.

I believe there was a part of me then that knew if I fell prey to panic, it would mean my demise. To look beyond the present was fraught with uncertainty. Each moment seemed to have an urgency that let me know I had no time to waste. Shelter for the night was the priority.

I began stacking small rocks under the overhang to build a low wall that would give me some shelter from the wind. More likely what it gave me was an illusory sense of safety that kept my mind from spiraling into despair.

I laid on the cold ground, the low wall of rocks to my left, the ledge overhead, engulfed in a vast wilderness. All light was nearly gone. The temperatures were dropping precipitously. Without the nylon jacket that was still tied to Jethro, I had on only a tank top and sleeveless acrylic vest. I pulled up the stretchy cotton tube skirt over my capri leggings so it covered my shoulders and arms.

I was totally unprepared for a November night in the high desert of northern New Mexico, where temperatures drop into the twenties and snow is not unusual at this time of year. My disappearance would not be known until I missed my physical therapy patient visits on Monday morning. There was no way to let anyone know what had happened. Jon, my dearest friend in Abiquiu, had dinner plans with another friend and was unlikely to try reaching me again, figuring Jethro and I were safe at home.

As the night grew darker and the temperature became colder, I instinctively pulled my knees to my chest trying to stay warm. Lying there, I began kicking my feet up and down to keep my blood flowing and my body temperature up.

There was no way I could sleep. My mind was more alert than it had ever been. Keeping myself moving was the only defense I had against the cold of the night. I pulled my vest up farther to cover my mouth and nose like a ski mask. I began a "breath of fire," a rapid yogic breathing in and out through the nose to generate internal body heat and fill the inside of my vest with the warmth of my breath. (Later, I would learn that the combination of moisture from my breath and the cold air of night could lead to potentially fatal hypothermia.)

I kept moving as the night grew deeper and the temperatures even colder. In the dark, I could hear Jethro whimper. The only condolence was that it meant he was alive. I called to him.

"Mama is here, baby."

"You are such a good boy."

"Look up at the sky, Jethro."

"Do you see the stars?"

"Night will pass."

"Morning always comes."

"I love you."

"I am here with you."

"Always."

Without food, water, or physical comfort of any kind, I had no tools to sustain me other than faith. I am not a religious person or churchgoer. I do not have faith in Jesus or any theological text. The faith that was being called on under the overhang that night was a complete and utter surrender to what was happening. I had no control over the immensity of my situation, no control over the temperature or weather. I felt lost amid the vastness of the high desert wilderness, nothing more than a human speck against the insurmountable force of Nature.

Surrender seemed my only option if I were to survive. It was not the surrender of giving up; it was a total acceptance of the moment, of what was happening in the here and now in a way I had never experienced before. The small cry of fear or any nagging worry was lost amid the blessed state of grace that held me through the night.

As the blackness unfurled, stars filled the night, many of them shooting across the sky.

"Did you see that, Jethro? Wow! Wasn't that beautiful."

The moon was nearly full, and the light that bathed the surrounding cliffs painted fleeting, ever-shifting images etched in stone. Ancient faces held in the mountain were shapeshifting through the night.

I had learned of the Apus, the spirits of the mountains, from the medicine men and women of the *Q'ero* people of the Andes. For nine years, I had traveled to Peru with a group of women I shared a mentor with, spending most of our time in the mountains in ceremony and receiving initiations to awaken the Divine Feminine. The Q'ero speak of the Apus, the mountain spirits, with the intimacy of a beloved. They live in balance and with respect for all living things, guided by reciprocity, or *ayni*, to create right relationships with the world around them. They understand the balance of nature—its power and its beauty—not as an abstract concept but as an embodied way of walking through the world. For the Q'ero, restoring ayni, or right relationship, with our planet is essential to our human evolution on Earth.

Although the mountain spirits were a fascinating cosmology while I was immersed in the Andes, the idea did not translate to my life back in the U.S. Mountains were foreign to me. I was born at sea level in New York City. As a child, I spent my summers in the Atlantic Ocean near my grandparents' bungalow on Long Island. I didn't know any mountains growing up, and certainly had never heard the word Apu before going to Peru.

Yet while I lay isolated and alone on a remote mountain in New Mexico, those were the teachings—once foreign to me—that I felt now deep in my bones. Bathed in moonlight, under a canopy of shooting stars, I endured conditions I had never imagined held by what I would soon learn was an Apu.

The night lost all sense of time. I was utterly alone and yet at the same time inextricably woven to a sense of being one with all things. I watched a kaleidoscope of changing images as the moonlight reflected along the ledges and crevices. It seemed as if veils of ancient stone were parting to let me look deeper into the recesses of the mountain. At one moment, the light appeared to rest. An image revealed itself in the stone. It was a face, not clearly defined or detailed, as if I was looking at a faded old lithograph on the side of the mountain. Although my eyes could see the image, I was aware of its power not by my visual perception but by a profound knowing deep in my bones that I was in the presence of a sacred, ancient wisdom. I was literally in the presence of an Apu.

I remember hearing words, not audibly but in a way I could understand. There are not many who have witnessed this, I was told. I could understand why I thought. I imagined there were few people who faced circumstances so extreme. The Apu presented me with a question:

"If you did not bring fear or worry to this situation, why do you take fear and worry with you anywhere?"

Even before I was aware of the presence of the Apu, I felt deeply held and profoundly protected despite my dire circumstance. No one knew where I was. The only thing keeping me warm in the harsh cold of a November night was pulling up my tube skirt around my shoulders, lying on my back with my knees against my chest, continuously kicking my legs up and down, and breathing rapidly into my vest. But this deep sense of being held wiped away any fear or worry. Fear is my baseline, my resting state, the place from which I build my life. If I was not afraid here, when there was so much reason to be, why am I afraid anywhere?

I was astounded that under these harsh and extreme conditions—the wilderness, the bitter cold, the lack of gear and food, the separation from Jethro, the uncertainty of how this ordeal would end—I was not afraid. Nothing inside me felt attached to fear or worry. Once night descended, I was severed almost immediately from those constant companions, and this sudden liberation catapulted me into a state I had never experienced before.

Words feel too limited to express it, but if one comes close, it would be *awe*. The night sky, the stars, the ground beneath me—they all felt full of wonder, as if I had never seen or felt such things before. Each time I called to Jethro, it was as if to say *WOW*.

WOW to the Air.

WOW to the Sky.

WOW to the Earth.

WOW to the Universe.

It didn't matter what the specific was. Whatever I was perceiving had an aliveness, a newness, and a wonder in every moment as if I was experiencing it for the very first time. Fear and worry dissolved in this state of grace.

Moment by moment, breath by breath, the stars receded and made way for the dawn. The light of the new day let me begin my search to rejoin Jethro. He had stayed in the same spot, sitting upright with my nylon jacket still tied around his collar. Although I hadn't been able to lift myself out of the gully the night before, I knew I would find a way out. The certainty was absolute in a way that was new to me. I would reach Jethro. There was no doubt in my mind.

For an hour, I tried getting up on rocks to reach for anything sticking out of the ground above that I might be able to take hold of. Finally, I grabbed the trunk of a small sage bush. Only sheer will let me lift my body to higher ground. As I lay there, Jethro ran to me, yelping and jumping, panting, and licking. Through the night, I had heard him and reassured him as best I could, singing softly like a lullaby to help keep him safe. I was deeply grateful he had made it through the night. The Apu had held and protected us both. Once again, we began our ascent.

There seemed to be two choices: going higher to try getting back to the rim or finding a trail down along the mountainside. It had been over twelve hours since my last text with Jon. We talked every day, and I hoped he'd realize Jethro and I had not come home, but I didn't want to count on being rescued. I had no idea where I was, and could never imagine someone finding us in this vast remoteness anyway.

Jethro and I went higher and tried traversing until we found what looked like a friendly, tree-lined arroyo. There were tracks that looked like an elk had passed through. I have no experience in tracking but it seemed like any tracks, elk or otherwise would be good to follow: Wildlife travel here all the time; they would help guide us out.

The friendly arroyo turned menacing and ended at an impassable precipice. The trees stopped at the edge. There were no trails to lower ground beneath the rocky cliffs. Once again, we turned around and climbed up.

I turned on my phone and found I had been able to conserve enough power to send Jon a final text before it died. I told him we had spent the night and were heading down, and texted the landmarks I could see: Abiquiu Lake directly in front of me and the Rio Chama at 3 o'clock.

Even at this point, I was hesitant to ask for help. If I told Jon I needed help, it would mean the danger was real. I knew my personal demons about relying on others intimately: I didn't want to be a bother; I never felt there was anyone in my life I could truly count on; if I asked for help, it wouldn't be there anyway.

My best shot seemed to be to rely on myself, a life lesson learned the hard way. There had to be some way down. Depending on myself seemed like the only thing I could count on, so I was vague about how serious my situation was. Jon was left reading between the lines to realize my danger.

The last time I'd had anything to eat or drink was Sunday morning. Twenty-four hours had passed without food or water. I wasn't hungry, but my mouth was as dry as the desert. It was painful to swallow. I couldn't keep moving. Even small efforts were too taxing as the sun rose higher and the heat built up. I laid down in the shade and felt my heart beating against the Earth. Rest seemed to be the medicine I needed.

I changed my plan, deciding that a day of rest would give me the strength to climb again tomorrow. I knew there was no water anywhere on the mountain. Seeking shelter from the burning sun became the priority. I found a low-lying cypress and kept shifting as the day passed between a hollowed out side for shade and then the other to warm up again. Jethro appeared to need the rest as much as I did.

At some point, a sound seemed to break through the silent landscape. It seemed like a far-off echo in the distance. I looked down from the edge of the cliff at the mountains around me. Something flickered below, maybe sunlight reflecting off the mica in the rocks. There was no way to tell if anyone was there, but I yelled anyway.

"HELLO, I SEE YOU!"

I shouted again, waving my arms.

"HELP! PLEASE!"

I called until the effort seemed fruitless. I didn't know if anyone had heard, but I'd seen the flickering light move. I was certain it was another human being. Then the light stopped. It had moved out of my sight. There was no response to my yells. I walked back to the cypress and waited for the sun to set.

As daylight faded, I wrapped Jethro inside my tube skirt like a papoose. I kept moving and breathing but with much less vigor than the night before. Although I had two more layers now—my nylon jacket and Jethro—I felt colder. Then in the blackness, distant dots of light appeared. It was hard to tell if they were moving. I couldn't imagine what they were. There were no homes for miles and miles in any direction. Suddenly, in what seemed like the next moment, the faraway specks seemed to organize themselves side by side, moving slowly as if through molasses. A far-off caravan of lights was coming closer. Was it possible these lights were for me? Did someone know I was here? Did the flickering light I'd seen earlier mean someone had heard my calls for help?

I couldn't judge the time, but the lights eventually stopped moving. Then a single line of headlights replaced the caravan. As it neared the base of the mountain, I could hear voices.

"WE ARE SEARCH AND RESCUE. CAN YOU HEAR ME?"

"YES, I HEAR YOU!" I shouted.

"ARE YOU INJURED?"

"NO, JUST COLD," I called back.

I couldn't believe it. How did they appear out of the darkness at the base of the mountain where Jethro and I sat under a cypress tree trying to stay warm? They were too far away to reach me in the dark, but just knowing someone had found me was uplifting and energizing. At first light, they'd start up. I could make it through another night knowing there were others down below.

A couple of hours must have passed, then I heard voices behind me.

"CAN YOU HEAR ME?"

"CAN YOU SEE OUR LIGHTS?"

"YES! YES!" I shrieked incredulously.

I was much closer to the top of the mountain than the bottom. Were the voices behind me close enough to reach me tonight?

"We are coming. Stay where you are." The call rang through the dark of night, the unknown voices of angels. The enormity of my situation then hit me. At the words "We are coming," I began shivering uncontrollably. It was as if I could finally succumb to the gravity of my situation, knowing help was so near. My mind was swirling, unable to make sense of anything that was happening. How could anyone know I was here? How was it possible anyone could find me in the middle of the night? What had possibly led Search and Rescue to a woman and her dog sitting under a cypress tree in the blackness?

Voices kept calling out.

"We are coming."

"Can you hear us?"

I called back, "I'm here."

Four human figures emerged from the dark. For the first time since the hike began, I was in the company of others. Jethro had become more subdued through the ordeal but began barking ferociously when he saw the men, as if he needed to protect me from our rescuers. Their first words were, "You don't know how happy we are to see you!" They could not have been happier than I was.

There was a flurry of activity as they pulled off their backpacks and dug into them: hot tea from a thermos, granola bars and dried fruit, water and beef jerky for Jethro. They pulled out a hat and gloves. I was wrapped in a down jacket.

"Do you know what time it is?" a man asked.

"I have no idea."

"11:15."

I had no way of knowing how they'd found me. "I thought I saw a person yesterday," I said. "Are they the one who called for help? Will I be able to meet them? They saved my life."

There were so many questions. I was overwhelmed with gratitude for these strangers who had trekked through the dark of night, and for the stranger in the distance who must have called Search and Rescue. Maybe the flickering light I saw had been a person? It had to be the one who called for help.

"That was your friend Jon," they told me. "He was incredible in helping us find you." I later learned he had been the person I saw moving in the distance. He had hiked in with food and a gallon of water, thinking he would meet us on our way out. He'd been calling my name. The flickering light was the sun's reflection on the water jug, a golden orb held high in one hand as Jon waved it back and forth. He had told Search and Rescue he thought he saw someone on the ledge but couldn't be sure.

Though the Search and Rescue team had tents and was ready to stay the night if I couldn't hike out, I was revitalized by their support and ready to leave the ordeal behind me. With headlamps, topographic maps, and a lifeline to the Command Unit below, we arrived at their base camp at 3 o'clock in the morning.

Teams of people were waiting at the camp. I remember asking, "Who does things like this for other people?"

"Retired military, ma'am," I was told. It did feel like I had been part of a tactical operation beyond anything I could have imagined. I remember one of the commanders telling me that conditions during the night were a perfect trifecta. Whatever ledge I was on had acted like a mountain amphitheater making it possible for me to hear their calls and for them to hear my responses. And there was no wind, so our voices could carry through the silence.

A miraculous matrix of events occurred that night that led Jethro and me off the mountain. Years earlier, a shaman in Peru had told me I must write a book. "The Apus will help you," he said.

I'd had no idea how the Apus would help me. Until now.

I have come to see the spiritual journey of my life much like climbing a mountain. There have been many struggles to overcome and challenges to rise above. In this way, it has been a climb. But the climb, I have learned, is not a competition to see who can get there first. The climb is not about conquering the mountain.

So why climb? Why begin the ascent at all?

Because when we get to the summit, we can see in all directions. The spiritual journey that brought us there allows us the widest possible perspective. We can see what is above and what is below. Our vantage point is elevated, our vision is broadened. We climb in order to see, wide and clear.

Enlightenment is like that.

CHAPTER TWO

The Prophecy of a Coca Leaf

ON THE OUTSKIRTS OF CUSCO in a rustic hotel in Peru, I met Don Andreas, a medicine man from Q'ero. As I entered the sparsely furnished room off the wraparound second-story balcony, he greeted me with a broad smile that immediately put me at ease. A colorful beaded *chullo*, an Andean alpaca hat, sat atop his head, with red and pink tassels hanging from each ear flap. A hand-woven poncho draped his shoulders in bright colors and geometric patterns. He ushered me to sit across from him at a wooden table covered with a hand-woven textile. The tiny uncovered windows on the back wall let in the afternoon light. I had scheduled a coca leaf reading with this shaman of the Andes before my arrival.

This was my third trip to Peru. About twenty women from all parts of the United States and Canada began making the trek in 2009 as part of our commitment to the Earth and the Divine Feminine, rebalancing the masculine and feminine within us. We always spent a few days in Cusco to acclimate to the altitude before heading into the mountains. Many of the women arranged for coca leaf readings or soul retrievals with the shamans we traveled with before we began our trek to the Andes.

As we sat across from each other, Don Andreas took a sip of floral-infused ceremonial water. He sprayed it from his mouth in each of the four directions to create sacred space, then took a number of coca leaves in his hands. He began blowing into the leaves—a sacred plant medicine that shamans in Peru use for healing, ceremony, and divination—while praying in Quechua, a language native to the Q'ero. He asked me nothing. After a few moments, he haphazardly threw the leaves on the table. Don Andreas lifted his head, looked me in the eyes and asked, "Did you write a book?"

My jaw dropped. How could this shaman from the remote mountains of Peru know something so specific about me, about my obscure self-published book? I had written *A Structure for Spirit* a few years earlier as a guidebook to help create a daily practice. There was no way he could have known anything about it. And yet he had not asked about something general like family or faith but a particular thing I'd done that not very many other people did. For him to see something in those scattered coca leaves was astounding.

"You have to make it bigger," he said. "You have to include more of what you have learned on your journeys here in Peru. You are like a farmer planting seeds that others may harvest in the future. This wisdom is not your own. It must be shared. The Apus will help you."

I had no thought of ever writing a book again. I did not even consider myself a writer. And even if I did decide to write another book, how on Earth would the Apus help me? The idea that I had a book to write left me shocked and a bit overwhelmed. It was the furthest thing from any plans for my life, but if a shaman from the holy mountains of Peru tells you to write a book, you really should start writing.

The next day, our group headed to the mountains: twenty women and four shamans piled into two minivans on the way to Apu Salkantay. Somewhere along the hairpin turns, our drivers pulled over. We climbed out and began walking higher to find a site for the most sacred ceremony of the Andes; the *despacho*. We sat in a circle as the shamans laid woven textiles on the ground. A piece of wrapping paper was placed on them to hold our prayers. With red and white carnations on each side of the paper representing feminine and masculine energies, we began to blow our prayers into coca leaves.

I thought of the delight I felt blowing wishes into dandelion seeds as a child. Dreams were set free in the wind, scattered to unknown places over all the Earth. There was never a worry about how a dream would happen. There was no fear about not having enough resources to make the dream come true. The wish was made from the innocent heart of a child. The shamans taught us that our heart was the most important element of ceremony. We are all, at our very heart, a shaman, connected to Earth and Spirit.

Once the coca leaves were placed atop the bed of red and white carnations, our prayers were fed with offerings of sweets and grains, corn and wine. The wrapping paper was folded over the sacred contents and tied up like a gift. We carried the despacho with us as we continued our trek to Apu Salkantay. It was an offering to the mountain before our arrival.

As we began our hike down from 12,000 feet after the ceremony, I experienced the Earth in a way I'd never imagined possible. A surge of energy was coursing up to my underbelly and dropping back down into the earth, creating a circular loop of power that propelled me down the mountain. I began to run, fast and effortlessly. I couldn't hold back. I had been running for many years, so running was not unusual for me, but the energy that fueled me then was like nothing I had ever felt before.

I was thrust into an unstoppable stride, as if the power of a stallion was running through me. I became keenly aware of how four-legged animals move so effortlessly across the earth, with the same power I felt running wild and free within me. Wild animals aren't distracted by mindless chatter as they charge on ahead, they're not competing to reach their destination; they are in deep communion in the most intimate of connections with the divine life force pulsing beneath them. They are fed by the Earth. They are sustained by her. They open up without restraint, again and again, in an ongoing dance of majesty as they run free. By the time I reached the base of the mountain, all I could do was bow to the ground and kiss the Earth in a cascade of tears. To taste but a drop of that divinity was spontaneously humbling. To receive but a small cup of that elixir was a touch of grace. Pachamama was fueling me with the fortitude I would need to fulfill a prophecy.

It has been many years since I felt the power of a stallion running through my body as I did that day on the mountain. As a practice, I still draw that power into my body through my intention and breath. Imagine roots running from the bottom of your feet reaching deep into the earth as you stand on the ground, or extending from your pelvis if you are sitting.

The Earth sustains all life on this planet and provides everything we need in order to thrive. Imagine pulling that life force into your belly. Allow yourself to receive whatever you may need in order to heal and replenish yourself. As you exhale, imagine any dense or heavy energies dropping back into the Earth where they can be broken down and composted. Even a few minutes of this practice will deepen your relationship to Pachamama, our Earth Mother. This power from the Earth pulses continuously. We are the ones who unplug. For those who are aware of the connection, it is one that forever deepens, for the heartbeat of our Earth Mother is boundless.

CHAPTER THREE

Dimming My Light

I WAS BRIGHT AS A young girl. I scored well beyond my grade level on all the standardized tests. School subjects came easily. Through every quarter of every year in elementary school, I received straight A's. I was the only one to get a medal for academic excellence at the award ceremony at the end of sixth grade. I did not aspire to be smart. It came naturally. I didn't give it much thought.

In 1972, I entered seventh grade. Sitting there among the neat rows of desks, I stared at the test paper the teacher had just passed out, and, pencil in hand, deliberately began to mark in the wrong answers. I did not want high marks. I did not want to be known as a smart girl. Somehow, I had come to believe that a boy would not like a girl who was smarter than he was. At twelve years old, I wanted a boy to like me. I dimmed my light and dumbed myself down to get that boy, whoever he was. It was a pattern that would continue throughout my life, in all my intimate relationships with men.

No one ever directly gave me the message that boys don't like smart girls. Although I remember consciously marking in the wrong answers to lower my test scores, I was unaware of what was driving me to do so. The smart girl theory was an insidious transmission downloaded into my twelve-year-old psyche from a culture in which men held the power. I saw this in my home and, even to my young eyes then, in the world around me.

Coming of age in the '70s meant I was wedged between two generations of women. The era before me was the one in which my mother and grandmothers shaped their lives around home and family and surrendered the power of finances and money to men. Ahead of me, the modern feminists were emerging, with their fight for equal rights and equal pay, hailing Helen Reddy's "I Am Woman" as their anthem. *Our Bodies, Ourselves* was the pioneering oracle bringing the previously taboo topics of women's health, sexual independence, and reproductive rights to the masses.

I saw my mother as miserable in her marriage. Her sobbing sessions behind locked bathroom doors were a normal part of our life. While Mom sat on the toilet seat, I stood next to her, absorbing her sorrow to let her misery dissipate and keep her in the marriage. Perhaps it was my responsibility as the oldest of five. At the heart of her agony was my dad's drinking.

"Life would be wonderful if only your dad would stop drinking," was her elusive dream for our family.

My mother's heartache was painful to see. I was powerless to make any change. I was confused and often angry hearing about her unhappiness and how much she hated my dad's drinking. I had no consolation to offer, no sage advice at eight years old. My sole purpose through those merciless laments was to listen. Once my mom had exhausted her tears, the bathroom door would open, we would walk into the hallway and nothing ever changed.

One day, tortured by sitting through another crying session, I burst out with: "Just leave him!" Her response left an indelible imprint on my life. "Your father brings home a good paycheck," she said. My dad was a traveling salesman. He sold perfume and cosmetics to department stores in and around New York City. He had dropped out of college to start supporting a family when my mom became pregnant with me. I remember the vow I made to myself in that moment: Never would I depend on a man for money. What my mother had said was a frightening window into the world of grown-ups. I could see even then that whoever had the money held the power. Perhaps it was no surprise that the will of my eight-year-old self was not strong enough to surmount the psychological imprint my mother's misery would leave on me. Later in life I would find myself right where I said I would never want to be.

My search for love as a young woman was grounded in the belief that I had to give my body away for someone to love me. Love and sex were entangled in a confused kinship severing my heart from my sexuality. My search for love involved cruising Long Island bars on weekends listening to local bands play deafening covers of Bon Jovi, Journey, and Foreigner.

Screwdrivers were my drink of choice, starting even before I left home. With the bathroom door locked, I covered my lids in heavy blue eye shadow and separated my mascara-laden eyelashes with a safety pin. Between sips of vodka and orange juice, I was blowing out my hair to slay the frizzy curls. Vodka was always in the pantry. Martinis were my dad's drink of choice.

Screwdrivers were my drink throughout the night. Many bars offered "two-for-one" specials or "Ladies Night," which meant you didn't have to pay for drinks at all. Numbed by alcohol, in a smoke-filled bar, screaming my name into someone's ear to be heard over the band was how an intimate evening started. This is where I found my first lovers. One-night stands, never to be seen or heard from again.

I remember a guy named Tony. He was a Merchant Marine I met at an East End bar known for heavy drinking, rock bands, and all-night partying in the summer. After a few hours of drinking and grinding to rock covers, we ended up in the back seat of his car. I don't remember much about the sex that night, but I do remember the question he asked me: "Did you come?" I had no idea what he was talking about. "Come where?" I thought. The question seemed to have some sexual relevance. Not wanting to seem ignorant, I answered, "Yeah." After all these decades, I remember the shame I felt lying through my alcohol daze. I wanted to act like I knew what I was doing when it came to sex.

My father liked to drink. It wasn't until much later in life we heard the word alcoholic in our house. It was probably around the time my mom joined Al Anon. When the word alcoholic was used, it was always in the context of our dad having a disease, a disease known as alcoholism.

Dad was a fancy drinker. He drank his martinis out of a wide-mouthed glass with a pickled onion or a cocktail olive dropped inside. His drinking was a trigger that changed the bearings in our home long before his eyes had a chance to glaze over. The moment the pantry door opened to pull the vodka bottle off the shelf or ice cubes were heard clinking in the shaker, my mother became despondent. Her voice ramped up to a high-pitched rage. She snapped easily at any question or remark. It was best to steer clear of her when Dad started drinking, which was a regular event in our home.

One thing my father liked when he was drinking was affection. After a few martinis, he would ask for a hug. If I whined about it or tried to say no, my father griped, "I work all week so you can live in this house and have food on the table and all I ask for is a hug from my daughter!" By this time, his speech was slurred. His eyes were bloodshot. I succumbed. I hated his smell. He reeked of alcohol and cigarettes. My body froze to tolerate the nauseating stench that engulfed me. Every muscle tightened in a shield of armor to ward off the guilt, the shame, the disgust of having my father hold me for way longer than I wanted.

The manipulative price tag on his affection became a high cost to get the love I wanted. The belief that I had to give my body away for someone to love me was imprinted at a young age and came to drive my earliest searches for love in the bars of Long Island. I wanted my father to love me, but those first expressions of affection toward me made me feel that I had no voice, no power, no say in what was allowed or not allowed in relation to my body. My words had no meaning. If I tried to say no, I felt guilty because all my father wanted was a hug.

I learned to keep quiet.

I learned that my words did not matter.

I learned I had no power over my body in relation to a man.

I learned that the way to get love was to give my body away.

As I look back from decades later, the lessons of those years seem like an example of how much pain and suffering love has caused in our world. But, of course, it isn't really love that's the cause; it's all the things that people—most of them women—have done or sacrificed in the name of love.

How do we learn about love? Is it from people who really know anything about it? Have you ever been punished and told it was being done out of love? Do you remember what messages about love you received as a child? As a woman, what was the relationship with your dad like? How has that influenced your relationships with other men?

When we look deeply, it's clear that we all hold both the feminine and masculine within us, regardless of what our bodies are. In my own childhood, the lesson was that goals and accomplishments were the measure of success. Feelings were not valued and were often punished. The threat of violence if they were expressed made me keep them hidden. And yet the feelings deep in our bones are the fullest expression of our feminine essence. From very early on, I learned that the masculine aspects of doing were much more important than the feminine aspects of feeling.

Bringing these aspects of masculine and feminine back into balance starts with awareness. Begin to notice if the masculine-driven principles of doing and achieving are driving your life at the expense of what your intuition or feelings may be telling you. Do you dismiss your intuition or gut feelings altogether? The whisper of our intuition needs stillness in order to be heard and felt? Give it that stillness. Find a time when you know you will not be disturbed. Lie back and let your body rest. Place your hands over your heart. Close your eyes. Cover them to deepen the darkness.

Allow your body to rest completely. Allow yourself to feel deeply supported. Let yourself be restored by the unconditional love and unwavering support of our Earth Mother. In a state of deep rest, you can ask her for a gift to help support your feminine essence. It may appear as an image, such as a flower or crystal, or might come through in words. Place your hands over your belly to bring this gift deep within. Return to it often, this gift of the Divine Feminine, when you are struggling or need healing, in whatever way feels natural for you. You can create a physical manifestation of your gift as something to wear or place on an altar. As with any gift, always hold it with gratitude.

CHAPTER FOUR

Running a Marathon

I HAD NO IDEA WHEN I began my first stumbling steps to physical therapy school that they would end up intertwining my work with my personal healing throughout my life. Little did I know that they were a calling to a better version of myself. Physical therapy has been more than my job but rather a mission that has provided countless opportunities for me to help uplift the world by uplifting others. I used to believe it was my job to fix someone and make them better. Meeting others at a time of crisis has taught me to hold an innate desire for them to be well and whole. For me, that has meant finding a spark, a quality each of us possesses, and amplifying that light in order for them to see the power of their own healing potential.

I started smoking at eleven years old. My dad was a heavy smoker. Cigarettes were easy to find. I started by stealing the red and white flip top boxes of Marlboros from the cartons that were always lying around our house. A missing pack or two went unnoticed.

When I first started breathing cigarette smoke into my lungs, I wanted to throw up. Although starting so young may seem unusual, many of my friends were smoking too. Perhaps it was a sign of the times back then, or maybe I liked the grown-up feeling, but something about smoking kept me at it. By the time I was thirteen, I was hooked. My habit was up to a pack a day. I smoked whenever and wherever I could, including in my high school bathrooms along with other classmates who were smokers too.

To hide the habit at home, I locked myself in the bathroom, stood on the edge of the bathtub, and blew smoke out an open window. I flushed the butts down the toilet and gargled with Listerine before unlocking the door. My habit eventually worked itself up to two packs a day, a chain smoker lighting my next cigarette with the end of the first before stubbing it out.

I first heard the words physical therapy from my Aunt Lilyan. She was my father's youngest sister, ten years older than me. We lived together for a short time in my early 20s at my grandparents' two-story attached home on 45th Street in Astoria, a working class neighborhood in Queens known for its authentic Greek food. I had moved into the finished basement because it was closer to Manhattan than my parents' house. My family had lived there when I was young before buying a Colonial-style home in a new community on Long Island. It was a source of pride for our family that Dad had achieved the American Dream: He had moved us out of the city and bought a home in suburbia.

With my grandparents spending the winter at a Florida mobile home park, Aunt Lilyan and I were the only ones at the house on 45th Street. I remember her telling me about a friend of hers: "Don graduated from school for physical therapy, and he said jobs are really easy to find." I had never heard of physical therapy before, but the idea of finding a job easily appealed to me.

Dad had drilled into us the future he insisted on: "You're going to college!" was a regular proclamation in our home. There were no discussions about how to pay for it or what we should study, but it was certain that we were going. Dad wanted to see his children live out the dream he hadn't been able to do himself.

After high school, I went to Suffolk Community College on Long Island and graduated with an associate's degree in social science, with the thought of becoming a social worker. I didn't know anyone who was a social worker and wasn't even sure what they did, but my idea of the job was that I would go into people's homes and make their families better. Fixing people's families appealed to me though it was actually my own I wanted to fix. I never became a social worker. Instead, I went to the Long Island Bartending School after I graduated (perhaps influenced by my familiarity with alcohol) and learned to make cocktails. My first bartending job was at a dive bar reeking of stale beer with a slight tinge of urine. It was small and dark, and your shoes stuck lightly to the floor with each step. The only customers were hard-drinking men who sat on stools on the other side of the bar while I filled their mugs with tap beer and served shots of Jack Daniel's.

After passing a customer a beer on tap once, I remember him telling me, "You smell nice."

Innocently, I replied, "I took a shower before I came."

"Do you shower after you come?" he taunted.

My breath stopped. There was that word again. I still didn't know what it meant, but I understood the sexual provocation. I tried to keep the shame and embarrassment from rising to my face as it had the first time someone asked me if I'd come. I didn't want to show how humiliated I felt while pretending to be cool with this kind of brazen sex talk from a stranger.

After that job, I went to work as a bartender for Sky Chefs at Kennedy Airport, which is in Queens like my grandparents' home. I was fascinated meeting travelers from Europe who wanted their beer at room temperature mixed with tomato juice or 7-Up—cocktails I never learned in bartending school. It was a huge step up from the dive bar I'd started at but short-lived since the job ended when air traffic controllers went on strike in 1981.

I would soon find myself typing in a little office near Rockefeller Center in Manhattan. As an administrative assistant for Kayser-Roth, a sleepwear company, I shared a tiny office just big enough for its two desks. One was mine and my electric typewriter's; the other, right behind, was my boss's.

I floundered through my early 20s with dead end jobs that took me from bars to department stores to typing in tiny offices. I remembered my inspiration to pursue physical therapy, based on the fact that my Aunt Lilyan had a friend who was one—and perhaps the impression my Aunt Tessie had left on me as a child, although I could not perceive it then.

Tessie was my grandfather's sister, and had been born with cerebral palsy. I saw pictures of her when she was young and still able to stand. As her life progressed, she lost her ability to walk and was ultimately confined to a wheelchair. When I was a child, she was living in an institution since our family could no longer care for her at home.

We would go to visit her on Welfare Island, which is what it was called until it was renamed Roosevelt Island in 1973. We drove over the bridge from Queens to Bird S. Coler Hospital on the little island in the East River. There, I would hold my grandfather's hand as we walked the dark halls to the room she lived in. The walls were bare except for the tiny windows covered in metal bars, making it feel more like a prison than a hospital.

What terrified me most on those visits were the people strewn through the hallways. Many were slumped in wheelchairs, held in place with belts, drool dripping from their open mouths. Others were lying on their backs strapped atop gurneys staring blankly at the ceiling. Indistinct groans bounced off the concrete walls and seemed to shout out the agony locked inside the twisted bodies, making it feel as if I was walking through halls of the living dead.

When we entered her stark room, with hospital beds lining the wall, my Aunt Tessie was the first sign of light. Her twisted smile and unintelligible grunts let us know how excited she was to see us. On top of the bedsheets was a worn piece of plywood no bigger than a modern-day laptop with chipped and faded letters of the alphabet painted on one side. With spastic movements, she pointed her twisted fingers at the faded letters to spell out words to try to convey the thoughts and feelings locked inside her. At five years old, it was a game I delighted in playing with her. Although the contorted body she inhabited destined her to such bleak and dire circumstances, she emanated light. In that light I was bathed in hope.

Later in life, hope was what pushed me forward when I finally decided I had to move past the dead end that my life had become, and began actually making plans to study physical therapy. Though I had an associate's degree in social science, I lacked the hard science courses I needed. To get them, I enrolled at Hunter College in Manhattan, fortunate that tuition was free because it was a city college. I knew I'd have to take out loans for the academic years to come. Staying in New York State was my only option since I couldn't afford the out of state living expenses anywhere else.

I made the waiting list of the State University at Stony Brook. With no other career prospects ahead of me, I used the next year to improve my science grades and get more volunteer experience, then reapplied. It was an esteemed program in the field, and I was fortunate that the director seemed to value my perseverance. I was accepted in 1986.

As I contemplated stepping into a health profession, I felt like an imposter. How could I be a healthcare professional if I myself was such a heavy smoker? I had tried to quit many times but never could do it for more than a day. Now, stepping into a health profession gave me a deeper motivation to stop, and also provided me with my first disciplined practice: running.

About a year before starting school for physical therapy, I had moved to the Upper West Side of Manhattan, sleeping on a friend's couch for $400 a month. My dad had gotten me a job as a "rotator" for city department stores, making more money than I had done typing. I went from one store to another spraying people with perfume or cologne. One day, I might be in Macy's spraying *L'Air du Temps*; another day, I could be at Lord & Taylor spraying a Pierre Cardin fragrance. Most people did not want to be sprayed. They ignored me completely. I spent my days standing in the middle of those crowded stores wearing a fake smile and extending a bottle of cologne that no one cared about to people who never knew I was there.

After work, I would walk through Central Park to get back to my couch. One day in early spring as the trees were erupting in green and horse-drawn carriages pulled tourists through the park, I noticed the runners. Men and women in sneakers, shorts, and T-shirts were rushing by me as they adroitly maneuvered their way around pedestrians, dogs, horses, and cyclists, undeterred by a city that never stops moving. Although I had seen them hundreds of times before, on this day, they stood out in a way they never had before. An unexpected well of tears spilled from my eyes and ran down my cheeks. I stood still in a bustling park as the life of the city whirled around me. I was nearly twenty-six years old. I was smoking two packs a day. The simple act of running was out of my reach. I could never imagine being able to do something like that. And yet, what these moving, vibrant people were doing seemed as if it might be the one thing that could actually help me stop smoking.

Knowing that physical therapy school would begin in a few months, I decided to start running. I really wanted to quit smoking, motivated by the career path I could see ahead of me. When I first began running, my lungs felt painfully stabbed by the air I gasped into them. Running made me nauseous too, just as smoking had at the start. The first thing I did after a run was light up a cigarette. Stopping my smoking habit was a slow and gradual process, but I kept running. In a moment of enlightenment, it became clear: I could not simultaneously be a smoker and a runner. I chose running.

A few months before P.T. school started, I left my friend's couch in the city to share a rental house on Fire Island, where I cleaned houses for the summer. The ferry from Patchogue took me to the hamlet of Davis Park and my home for the summer: the Piano House, named for the large upright sitting on the front porch. I can't imagine how that piano ever got there in the first place, since the ferry was the only way to the island and boardwalks were the only paths. The only way that piano could ever leave Fire Island would be in ashes.

There were twelve of us renting the Piano House that summer. Between house-cleaning gigs, I spent my time running along the shores of the Atlantic. By the time I started P.T. school, I was free of cigarettes.

I wish I could say I never smoked again, but there were lapses. Renée was the one other smoker in my class, and inevitably, we became friends. Whenever we got together, I ended up smoking. It was another moment of enlightenment when I was seized with the realization that if I wanted to stop smoking altogether, I had to cut Renée from my life. Our friendship ended.

The other kiss of kismet from P.T. school was meeting the man I would marry. My class was small, twenty-six students. We spent long days together in lecture halls and anatomy lab cutting up cadavers. We ate together, studied together, and partied together. I had a crush on Bobby, one of my classmates, but he had no idea I liked him. He never showed any interest in me and eventually started dating someone in the class who was younger and much cuter than I was. For one of our campus parties, Bobby invited Phil, one of his best friends who lived two hours away in Brooklyn and had recently graduated from the physical therapy program at Downstate Medical Center.

Phil stood out among our familiar crowd. He was tall and lanky with an athletic build, animated expressions, and a heavy Brooklyn accent. We spent most of the night talking. Before heading back to Brooklyn, he asked for my number. He said he would call, but I never expected to hear from him again. Over the years, I had given my number to plenty of guys who said they would call. None of them did. Except Phil. The next day, he called.

I was living with three roommates in a dorm at Stony Brook. Phil lived with a friend in an apartment off Ocean Parkway in Brooklyn, two hours away. I don't know how our relationship worked over that distance and time, but before I graduated from Stony Brook, he was my boyfriend. After I got my degree, his friend moved out and I moved in. It was not long afterward that Phil got down on one knee, opened a small box with a diamond ring, and asked me to marry him. The first thought that ran through my mind was: "I don't think anyone else will ever ask you again."

That's how little self-worth I had. Any sense of who I was, how I felt about things, or what it meant to be a woman was buried so deep it was hidden even from me. I could put on a good facade, but most of the time, it felt as if I was acting being in a relationship. I never knew what my true feelings were. I responded in ways that I thought I was supposed to. I didn't really know what love felt like. I'm not sure if I ever fell in love with Phil. I think I would have known if I had. When he asked me to marry him, I said, "Yes."

Phil and I were compatible. We were both physical therapists. We both liked the outdoors. We were both athletic, although he was much more so than me. I liked his family, and my family liked him. I had never dreamed of being married or pictured myself as a wife or fantasized about weddings. But I did know I wanted to be a mother. One thing was certain. Phil would be a great dad. It was not so much love that made me say yes but rather a sense of security. Phil was someone who called when he said he would call. He was there when he said he would be. Phil was a person you could count on. Isn't that why people get married? I didn't know much about love, but I think on some level, I wanted to feel safe. I didn't realize it at the time, but one thing was certain: Phil was safe.

By the time I met him, I was no longer smoking. A mile was as far as I'd ever run, but with Phil as my trainer as well as my husband, he inspired me to run the New York City Marathon. Were it not for him, I never could have imagined that running twenty-six miles was even possible. That's one of the reasons Phil's patients loved him. It was his innate nature to help push people further than they ever thought they could go. He had me running on a track which I'd never done a day in my life, but I loved it. Phil, with his own experience as a marathon runner, plotted out a training schedule, and he was my biggest cheerleader. The month before the marathon, I was running from our apartment in Park Slope over the Brooklyn Bridge and up through Manhattan to Central Park and then back home again—twenty-four miles. I'd never thought I could ever run that far.

The NYC Marathon begins on Staten Island. As we assembled at the start in the early morning freeze of November 5, 1990, I waited covered in a Hefty garbage bag, trying to stay warm. Tens of thousands of runners jockeyed for position. Being too far back in the pack could cost you time just getting to the starting line. Minutes were precious. I had been training not just to run twenty-six miles but to do it in three and a half hours or less. I remember Phil telling me before the race, "Be sure to get up front."

As we crossed the Verrazzano-Narrows Bridge to Brooklyn, I could feel it bouncing beneath the rhythmic, beating feet of 25,000 people. Pounding feet and heavy breathing were all I could hear as runners jockeyed to find their position and establish their pace. As we got closer to the end of the bridge, screams could be heard in the distance. When we entered Brooklyn, the roaring crowd seemed like it was sometimes a hundred people deep. It brought me to tears. Strangers were cheering on runners, offering high fives, taking the time to lift each one of us up as we started the long journey. Many of us had been preparing for months, even years. The love from the crowds was palpable.

As we ran on through the city, each neighborhood had its own character. Crowds were sparse in the Bronx. The Hasidic Jews in Williamsburg were reserved. The raucous yells of Bay Ridge and Long Island City were rowdy. Somewhere in the middle of Brooklyn, a band played the theme from *Rocky.* Never in my life had I felt so inspired by that song.

Distance runners talk about "hitting the wall," usually at about twenty miles in a marathon. Suddenly, the muscles have no energy left. But for me, it was the opposite. I just kept running, and at twenty-four miles, I had a breakthrough. After all those streets and bridges, all those heavy legs, burning lungs, and aching muscles, my body broke free of resistance. At Columbus Circle, heading into Central Park , anything that had previously weighed me down was gone. It suddenly felt as if I was floating through space. By continually pushing past my body's limits, I reached a dimension I had not known existed. Effortlessness flowed as resistance melted. After running twenty-four miles, I felt endless reserves of energy, like I could have run another marathon. After three hours and forty-one minutes, eleven minutes longer than my goal, I crossed the finish line in ecstasy. The time invested and the miles covered had all been worth it. My thighs hurt so much I couldn't climb stairs for a week, but I had done what I once thought was impossible.

Running was the first disciplined practice I ever established in my life. It was what ultimately restored my breath. You certainly don't have to run a marathon to establish a practice. It can be anything you integrate into your lifestyle that you continue with regularity—walking, dancing, or any other activity your body enjoys. Having a practice that moves my body each day has been cleansing for mind, body, and soul, letting dense or heavy energies pass through me more quickly. Find something that your body enjoys or that makes you feel glad you did it. Start small and set realistic goals. It can be as simple as going for a walk on a Saturday morning or putting on music and letting your body move at the end of the work week to shake out stress. Even running a marathon started with the first step.

CHAPTER FIVE

A Daily Practice

MY GRANDMOTHER'S BASEMENT ON 45TH Street in Astoria was an unlikely wellspring of enlightenment. She had grown up in the Depression. She counted her pennies, cut out coupons, and hoarded toilet paper. It was there that I discovered an obscure book, *Autobiography of a Yogi*. Most likely, it belonged to my Aunt Lilyan (from whom I also discovered the Beatles, *Magical Mystery Tour*). Lilyan would be much more likely than my grandmother to stash a book about a yogi.

As I thumbed through the pages, I was fascinated by pictures of this man from India shaping his body into positions I had never seen before. In one particularly vivid image, he was running a cloth between his nostrils, which I didn't know was humanly possible. It all seemed so foreign and exotic and otherworldly. Those may be the pages on which the word enlightenment first appeared to me. It was a word that propelled me to seek, symbolizing a destination, offering escape from misery into a world of perpetual bliss. Attaining this, in the way my mind conjured it up, always involved images of lone monks, always male, meditating in remote caves high atop mountains.

One of my many trajectories along the relentless road to enlightenment came from a New York City radio host, Armand DiMele. He hosted The Positive Mind on WBAI, which I could listen to on my car's AM radio. Armand had an uncanny, almost psychic, ability to see things in his callers. I was fascinated that he could tell so much about people just by talking to them on the air. The compassion he evoked through the airwaves made me trust him, which led me to begin therapy sessions in holotropic breathwork at the Positive Mind Center, which he had founded on West 57th Street in Manhattan.

Holotropic breathwork had been developed by Stanislav Grof, a Czech-born psychiatrist who devoted his career to exploring non-ordinary states of consciousness. After early research on psychedelics and the therapeutic potential of LSD, he went on to develop holotropic breathwork, a groundbreaking form of experiential psychotherapy. During holotropic breathwork sessions, you lie on your back and breathe for two to three hours. By altering your normal breathing pattern in particular ways, you bypass the often critical and judging mind. For me, the breath leads directly to the truth and wisdom held within the body, contrary to where thinking takes us.

My first session felt like tripping without psychedelics. Lying on my back with eyes closed and mouth open, I was instructed to breathe without pausing between the in-breath and out-breath. At times, I was told to breathe faster or more deeply, until rivers of pent up tears fell from my eyes, the source of the sorrow unknown. At some point, my awareness of breathing was gone. The breath had become a conduit that catapulted me into an altered state not bounded by time.

I remember being surrounded by mountains, elevated by their majesty. I remember watching an eagle soar through magnificent snow-capped peaks. At some point, I was no longer looking at the eagle but had become the eagle. I was traveling over mountaintops seeing the world below from a very high perspective. I remember feeling as if I had been lifted out of the confines of my physical body. I was no longer limited by a small mind and narrow beliefs. I felt expansive and liberated and free. This was the first of countless breathwork sessions in my life that offered a momentary taste of enlightenment. It was this taste that kept me seeking for some permanent state of Nirvana I could cling to.

Another pioneer in the field of body-centered psychotherapy was Dr. Alexander Lowen, known as the father of bioenergetics. His work focuses on how our energy flows between body and mind, and studies the muscular patterns that develop to handle the pain and stress of life. These patterns become anchored in the body, Lowen has found, and block us from expressing joy, pleasure, and creativity.

To have a session with Dr. Lowen, you had to send a letter stating why you wanted to see him. To me, surely someone so esteemed in his field would hold the cure to my misery. Enlightenment, I believed, was held by some magical person or in some mystical circumstance that had all the answers for my questioning mind. I chased so many methods and teachers that Phil often quipped, "Who's your guru this month?" I was continually seeking some outer authority who I believed held the key to my happiness.

I have no recollection of what I wrote in that letter to Alexander Lowen, but six months later, his office called: "There has been a cancellation. Can you be here tomorrow afternoon at 2?" It felt like winning the lottery. I dropped everything to be there. Lowen was nearly eighty when I saw him, but the ease and vitality in his body defied his years. Within a few minutes of my walking into his office, he looked me straight in the face, pulled down my eyelids, and said, "If I had to give you a diagnosis, I'd say you're scared to death."

"Impossible," I thought. "I'm never afraid." Years later, I realized that I was so terrified of my feelings that I was numb to any emotion, including fear. Yet Lowen could see, deep in my eyes, what I was blind to: a little child buried in the fear she would never be loved.

He then proceeded to have me lie backward over a padded bench with my feet on the ground and my arms and head hanging back. He encouraged me to breathe deeply. He told me to keep repeating the word "why" over and over. The word why seemed to unlock a reservoir of needs not met and questions unanswered, rocking my body in a torrent of sobs as I lay arched over the bench.

My right arm began flailing about. I had no control over its movements. I felt as if I was losing my mind, as if my body had betrayed me with its freakish behavior.

The next day, I couldn't move my shoulder. I thought I had done some serious damage during the session. It took a few days before I regained control over my arm again. That was the only time I saw Alexander Lowen. The brief therapeutic encounter left me bewildered. My armor had been cracked, and I didn't like the feeling. Only through the lens of time can I see the puffed up arrogant posture I was using to shield myself from feeling anything in my body, including fear. Fear had shaped me to the smallest denomination of myself so I could not be seen. It built a fortress of protection around my heart which so desperately wanted to keep pain out and ensure that nothing got in. Yoga, more than any other practice, has softened the tightened muscles that my mind had twisted into a relentless defense against the perception of an unsafe world. I never would have discovered this had it not been forced on me.

Sometime in the late '80s, I began taking classes at Kripalu, a retreat center in the Berkshires in Massachusetts where I was delving deeper into yoga, meditation, chanting, and trance dancing. I felt a freedom there that eluded me in the rest of my life. By this time, Phil and I were married, both working as physical therapists while contemplating moving out of Queens and starting a family. After spending a weekend at Kripalu, the drive home was usually spent in tears. I always tasted something authentic there that contrasted with the facade of the life I was returning to.

It was the Berkshires I returned to years later to train in Phoenix Rising Yoga Therapy, which I had heard about at Kripalu. I remember thinking that my career as a physical therapist might be shifted in a new direction by the program of yoga postures and a mirroring dialogue to heighten the awareness and wisdom in our body.

I began making the drive every month for the training. By this time, Phil and I had two young daughters. Although the certification in Phoenix Rising did not lead me to enlightenment or a new career path, it did give me the gift of sadhana, a daily spiritual practice. This was something that was required as part of our Phoenix Rising training, and a huge change from my previous practice of yoga. I took occasional yoga classes and stretched when I felt I needed it. Practicing yoga every day however caused a resistance to erupt that seemed insurmountable. Every morning, my mind tried to convince me that staying in bed was a better option than getting up to practice yoga. Anger would surge within me, raging against an authority that was telling me what to do. My mind stormed against the program and teachers for insisting on yoga practice every day.

I resisted.

Hard.

But I did it.

Despite the resistance, I woke before my daughters to roll out a yoga mat. I had no formal training but twisted my body into positions I'd learned from classes and books.

As I look back, I believe my lack of yoga training helped me listen to my body and trust that I would get what was needed from my morning practice.

In the beginning, I spent my time on the mat trying to cram as many different positions as possible into the thirty minutes or so I allotted. I never had time for savasana or corpse pose, in which you lie on your back at the end of the practice to let your body deeply relax and integrate the benefits, soaking them in like a sponge. I had better things to do than lie on my back and do nothing. My beliefs were still dominated by the patriarchal paradigm that valued doing over being, which was mirrored by my practice.

Despite the resistance and harried pace of my early practice, over time, the day-to-day ritual of coming to a mat each morning has slowly whittled away at the fear that kept me from seeing clearly. Yoga has brought me more deeply into my body by unraveling the tensions held in my muscles, tissues, and sinew—one breath at a time.

During the later years of my marriage, my yoga practice brought me to my knees each morning as the top of my head dropped to the mat. With my hands clasped behind my back, my arms rose overhead, deepening the connection of my head to the ground. Often, I would stay in this position for fifteen or twenty minutes. I had no choice. My head seemed magnetized to the Earth. My shoulders ached from holding the posture so long, yet I could not move of my own volition. At some point, my body would collapse into child's pose. I would sit back on my heels with my arms resting alongside my body. The pressure at the top of my head would roll to my forehead. The position was forcing me to bow to my heart and listen to its truth rather than be led by the fear in my mind. I didn't understand that my body was trying to enlighten me in ways I couldn't see until years later.

Over the years, my daily practice has been a reflection of my evolution. It has slowed down. Movement and breath have become prayer. I can count on one hand the number of positions my body is in each morning now. I spend more time in each posture, allowing my body to discover an awareness of something new in a shape it has taken for years. I always include savasana. My practice grounds my body and stills my mind so my prayers feel deeper, allowing me to drop a bit of good into the world. I offer gratitude for the blessings in my life. I call to my ancestors—many whose names I don't know—and loving allies on the other side to thank them for watching over my daughters, my family, and all beings. I pray for peace for our country and our world. More than twenty-five years later, I still start my practice each morning with my head bowing to my heart.

Our spiritual nature is the highest dimension of who we are. Any practice you commit to will fortify the connection with your higher being. A shaman who wants to create change will work at the source. Imagine a river flowing down a mountain. Someone looking to change the course of that river doesn't start where the river ends. Think of the labor of digging trenches, building dams, and working your way upstream to alter the flow of the river. The shaman starts at the source. The slightest change where the river starts completely changes its entire course down the mountain. Your spiritual practice is tending to that source—the source of your own river, your own Spirit, the highest source of your wisdom—to alter the course of where your life flows.

Each morning as I sit on bent knees with my legs folded under me and my spine straight, I imagine the light of peace spreading from my spine and filling my entire body. I imagine peace above me, peace below me, peace in front of me, peace behind me, peace to my right, peace to my left. Peace within me, peace around me. Surround yourself in whatever it is that you're looking to cultivate. I offer gratitude as I feel myself showered in the blessings of my life. This is what it means to tend to the source of our Spirit. This is what it means to work at the source of life. Even a few moments spent greeting the morning in this way can alter the course of how the river of your life flows.

CHAPTER SIX

One Step at a Time

THE FIRST TIME A MOUNTAIN spirit spoke to me was long before I ever heard the word Apu. Phil and I were newly married and living in Brooklyn. I had started my career in physical therapy at Rusk Rehabilitation Center in New York, which was known for its stellar reputation in the field of rehabilitative medicine.

Our honeymoon was spent in the Canadian Rockies, which astonished our friends and family. Most people head to a secluded beach resort or Caribbean island, but Phil had no interest in a typical honeymoon. His heart was set on the Canadian Rockies. He had recently been to the Olympic training center in Calgary with Paralympic athletes to whom he devoted an enormous amount of time throughout his life. He had wanted to go back, and our honeymoon gave him the chance to do that.

Other than a few high school ski trips to Hunter Mountain two hours north of New York, I had never been to the mountains. My native element was water, specifically salt water. My deepest kinship with nature as a child was the Atlantic Ocean. Growing up, I would visit my grandparents' bungalow a few miles from Smith Point Beach on the south shore of Long Island. Summers there were the brightest memories of my childhood.

My honeymoon with Phil was a far different world. By day, we hiked rugged trails amid turquoise lakes, majestic mountains, and receding glaciers. At night, we returned to luxury lodges and five-star dinners. After the exhilaration of our honeymoon, it was no surprise that Phil wanted to climb Mount Rainier a year later. Friends of ours had recently moved from Brooklyn to Seattle and thought it would be a great idea if we joined them to climb the highest U.S. mountain south of Alaska. Phil couldn't resist. As stunning as the Canadian Rockies were, this would be a much more dangerous adventure. I had fears about my abilities but went along with my husband's plans.

The company that would be leading the climb sent specific instructions on what to bring—climbing harnesses, ice axes, crampons, rigid mountaineering boots, gloves (and mittens to go over them), trekking poles, goggles, gaiters, headlamps, wool socks, thermal underwear, dehydrated food, Ziploc bags, toilet paper, water bottles, sunscreen, down jackets, and backpacks large enough to carry all the clothing, gear, and food. This trip was no honeymoon.

With everything packed in duffle bags, we flew to Seattle to meet our newly transplanted friends. As we started the day-long mountaineering school with them, most of us in the group were novice climbers—learning, among other things, how to stop ourselves with an ice ax arrest if we started sliding down the mountain. The first day's climb would take us to Camp Muir at ten thousand feet, where an overnight wooden hut was waiting, but we wouldn't be there long. Our ascent to the summit would start in the middle of the night so we could be there by sunrise. We would be roped in groups of four. If one person fell, the cry of "Falling" would signal the others to immediately drive their axes into the ice to keep the falling climber from taking everyone down with them.

We learned the rest step. With less oxygen at higher altitude, we were taught to take one step and stop, then another step and stop to conserve our breath and pace ourselves for the summit. The greatest danger was the crevasses, deep cracks in the ice that were often unseen because they were covered in snow, until someone stepped into one. Some that were well known had ladders over them that we had to step from rung to rung on to cross safely.

Learning those rudimentary skills offered some reassurance before we set out the next day, but I tried not to think too much about what lay ahead, focusing instead on the time with our friends.

After our day in the mountaineering class, we headed to a coffee shop to talk about what to expect on our climb up Mount Rainer the next morning. We sipped lattes and chai tea at a Seattle based coffee shop I'd never heard of named Starbucks. "These would do great in New York!" our friend Bill said. By the following year, you could find a Starbucks on nearly any corner in Manhattan.

The next morning, Phil and I, along with Bill and his wife, Trish, gathered at the base of Mount Rainier in T-shirts and light jackets to meet our guides and the dozen or so other climbers. It was a clear and sunny August morning as we began our gentle climb through the meadows of wildflowers and tall grasses. With trekking poles in hand, I could feel my heart race, anticipating the adventure ahead. An older couple quickly overtook us—well-known Rainier climbers from Austria who did the ten thousand feet up and back to Camp Muir a few times a week. Seeing these people twice my age easily doing what I was setting out to try boosted my confidence. If they were out here climbing, I had no worries I could do it too. That was how I started out, with an arrogance that time would make clear.

As we climbed, a light drizzle began falling, which is not unusual in the Northwest. We stopped to adjust our gear and continued on. As we climbed higher the rain turned to snow, the wind picked up, and before long, we were hiking through a blizzard—in August. As snow whirled around me, I could not see beyond it. Before long the snow was a foot deep as we trudged ahead. Conditions felt perilous. My mind raced with fear. How would I get off this mountain? The climb up was steep. Snow and ice covered everything, leaving no traction on the slippery slope. Sliding seemed like the only off ramp down; and down and down and down. The only options my mind could envision were being stuck on the mountain forever or plummeting to my death.

The wind became so loud we couldn't hear one another. We kept moving without respite, invisible to each other, determined to reach Camp Muir. I felt isolated and alone on an increasingly hostile mountain. The howling fear and growing panic were my only companions. I was certain death was near.

Suddenly a jolt seemed to knock the stampeding thoughts from my mind. My brain went blank. A stillness filled the space that had been spinning out of control. It was my first encounter with an Apu.

I heard words that seemed to drop into my head like pearls from somewhere outside me: "Follow the step in front of you. That is all you have to do. Just follow the step." I had never climbed a mountain before. I knew nothing of mountain spirits or Apus. But I knew the imprint of the climber's boot ahead of me as it sank into the snow. That was my only focus. Although I couldn't see the climber who made it, I could see that mark showing me the way. And so it was, boot print by boot print, one step at a time, we reached Camp Muir.

It was nothing more than a wooden hut with slatted bunks that would hold us until we started up again. It was shelter, a place to shed wet clothes and drink warm beverages in the heat of a woodstove. I was beyond grateful. I'll never know if the other climbers were as panicked as I had been. I told no one. I thought they'd think I was crazy, or—worse yet—unqualified to be there. I pretended that I knew what I was doing.

To reach the summit at sunrise, four thousand vertical feet away, we would begin our ascent at 2 a.m. We knew, above all else, that we must follow our guides' instructions implicitly. Once we stepped beyond Camp Muir, we were not at any point for any reason to veer off the path they led us on. Stepping in a snow-covered crevasse would mean death.

I had no sense of time. The altitude, the tight quarters at Camp Muir, the overwhelming climb made sleep impossible. The guides urged us to drink warm fluids. A few hours passed, and we began gathering our gear to start the ascent, layered with wool and down, gloves and mittens and gaiters. Stepping out of the hut in the middle of the night at ten thousand feet, the highest point I had ever been on Earth, felt like touching heaven. The sky was darker than I had ever seen it. Twinkling light filled the crystal-clear night from galaxies farther than I could ever imagine. I had never seen so many stars in one place at one time.

There was only silence and the sounds of breath and crunching snow. No one in our groups of four could be roped with a loved one, so no family suffered the loss of multiple members should a tragedy occur. We began our ascent to the summit with the light of stars above and headlamps strapped to our foreheads shining light on the ground below.

For two thousand feet, we kept on in the clear, cold silence. As the sky lightened, with the sun still hiding, our guides stopped. This is as far as we go, they said. Yesterday's storm had left conditions too difficult to continue in the two thousand feet that remained, three to four hours of hard climbing. It seemed tough to believe that we trekked up through a blizzard the day before, but now, in crystal clear conditions, we could go no farther. We were not a group of skilled climbers. We did not doubt our guides' judgment that we could not safely cross the ice-covered precipices ahead.

A blanket of relief enveloped me. The arduous struggle was over. I was greeting this new day, this new sun, on the top of the world.

Phil was gravely disappointed. He had come to the mountain to get to the top. For me, the journey had been enough. Phil did return a few years later and reached the summit. My first encounter with an Apu left an indelible imprint on my mind. One step at a time. That is all you have to do.

As I'd seen the older climbers setting out to do what I had come for, I had no doubt I could conquer this mountain. Only time has enlightened me to see the arrogance and superiority in my approach. As the shamans know and teach us, this is not the way to come into right relationship with a mountain. We must humble ourselves before it, for the mountain can crush us. One wrong step, one wrong move, and a mountain can end your life.

True power does not need to announce itself, or preach a long sermon to prove its worth. Humility is at the core of every power. Years later, traveling with the medicine men and women through the Andes, we created our offerings to the mountain, our despachos, before we went. Along the way, we built apuchettas, small shrines of rock and stone to offer our thanks. Time has enlightened me to the rightness of the reverence in which the shamans hold the mountains.

We as humans have walked on our Earth as if we have dominion over Nature. We must learn to be humble. We must walk, in the practice of Thich Nhat Hanh, as if kissing the Earth with our feet. When I walk in this way, a smile rises inside. I slow down. I am mindful of the contact my feet are making with the Earth. If each of us walked in this way, for a few moments a day, perhaps we could change the world. One step at a time.

CHAPTER SEVEN

Sinners and Saints

I DO NOT IDENTIFY WITH any religion. My father was raised in a Catholic church in Queens, but our religious upbringing was the work of my mother. Though she was raised in an Episcopal church in the Bronx, she took us to a Catholic church when we were young. I don't know if she converted or if my parents ever talked about the matter. It may have had more to do with my father's mother, who was a fierce and devoted churchgoer.

My grandmother was a diminutive woman, but when you went to church with her, she was larger than life. What stood out more than anything else about going to church with my grandmother was her voice. It was shrill and high-pitched, and pierced the high ceilings above all the other parishioners. She loved singing the church songs, and it didn't matter at all that she couldn't carry a tune. Her devotion to the church was wholehearted, and singing was an expression of that devotion. I imagine my grandmother had a big voice in deciding what church we went to.

Palm Sunday was the only day I enjoyed going to church as a child. On that day we came home with an origami-style cross made of twisted palm that would become a decorative wall hanging in my bedroom. Then there was Ash Wednesday, a black smudge of ash was smeared on my forehead that you were not allowed to wash off. It had to fade naturally. I didn't know what it was for, but it marked me as a Catholic. It reminded me of another black spot: the one my grandmother would find on my tongue.

If my grandmother thought I was up to some anti-biblical mischief. she would ask me to stick out my tongue. If she saw a black spot—which she always did—it was God's confirmation that I had in fact sinned. The black spots marked me as no good in the eyes of the Lord. They chipped away at any sense of worth before God. They deemed me shameful and inferior.

Then there was the confession booth—the ritual that brought me the most terror. We entered a tiny room, its musty smell infused with the sweat and sobs of the thousands of people who had crammed into this small space filling the air with the scent of their sins. There was a pad to kneel on and a small opening in the wall that was closed when you entered. On the other side of the wall sat the priest. Once you were inside, the small mesh covered partition would slide open. The priest sat far back enough on his side of the booth to avoid being seen by the sinner who was kneeling before him. He would break the silence by asking about my sins. The assumption was always I always had sins.

The mantra I recited was: "Forgive me, Father, for I have sinned. It has been two weeks (or whatever the lapse) since my last confession."

"I had a fight with my brother."

"I talked back to my mother."

"I stole Hostess cupcakes from the kitchen pantry when no one was looking."

"I lied about doing chores."

The sins of a child.

A punishment was doled out. "Say five Hail Marys and two Our Fathers," ordered the priest, and the little window would slam shut. I would leave the tiny sin chamber and kneel in a pew to repeat the prayers the priest had laid out to redeem me from my sins.

The church was mammoth, St. Joseph's in Ronkonkoma, with ceilings that must have soared four stories high. Stained glass windows flooded the space with prisms of light. Sunday mornings were a chaotic cacophony of my mother's shrieking commands to get us there.

"Get up!"

"Hurry and get dressed!"

"What is taking you so long?"

"We're going to be late!"

"Don't give me that look!"

"Stop yelling!"

The only one yelling, though, was my mother hurrying to get us out of the house and into the car. Rarely, if ever, did my father join us, though I don't know how he escaped the torture. My mother must have thought giving us religion was part of her job just like cooking dinner and washing clothes.

It was always a mad rush to get five young children dressed in their Sunday clothes out the door. My sisters and I were always in dresses, and my brothers in button-down shirts and slacks. I hated Sunday clothes. Besides being uncomfortable, they were like stepping into a skin that wasn't my own, pretending to be something I was not. I felt like an imposter sitting in a pew, reciting prayers as if we were some holy people when all our time was spent fighting to get there. We seemed to live in two worlds growing up. One that was presented to the outside world and one that we lived behind the walls of our home. Maybe that is true for all families.

The priest stool high above everyone else preaching martyrdom as the path to salvation. Altar boys stood around him swinging small censers of burning incense. Girls were never seen on the altar. The only women who had anything to do with church were the Sunday school nuns who would get us ready for a religious rite of passage like our first communion. All I remember about the day you got to eat one of those dry wafers for the first time was how hard it stuck to the roof of my mouth after the priest placed it on my tongue. It made me want to gag, feeling like my stomach would roll right up into my throat.

The other important aspect of rehearsing for our communion mass was making sure we knew the right answer to the question we'd be asked. The priest would look out over the congregation—all the girls sitting together looking like child brides in their white communion dresses—and ask, "How many girls want to be nuns when they grow up?"

All the hands around me went up. I was terrified. I knew I did not want to be a nun. What would happen if I didn't raise my hand? If I did, would that automatically make me a nun when I got older? Would lying in church have to be part of my confession? I remember the torment of agreeing to something I wanted no part of. The shame of being the only one not to raise my hand was more than I could bear. My hand went up with a power that was not my own.

Everything about church filled me with fear. I imagined God as a man overseeing the world from a throne high up in heaven. He had X-ray vision, being God of course, and could see straight to my soul where he would find every flaw, sin, and wrongdoing I was guilty of. I do not look back on anything I received from church as helpful. As a child, I felt afraid and never good enough. It seemed that God was always looking down on me and it filled him with disgust.

Decades later, as Phil and I were planning our wedding, his older sister had married for the second time and converted to Hasidism, the ultra-Orthodox Jewish sect. Women's roles are designated to the household while bearing many children. Men's role is study and prayers. The conversion was complete once she changed her first name, put on a wig, and wore long-sleeve dresses that hung well below her knees.

Phil had not been raised in a religious home. His family was more culturally Jewish than religious. Conversations around the dinner table in his parents' second-story Brooklyn apartment would inevitably lead to talk about Israel. His mother was intimately aware of what was happening in that part of the world. On the other hand, Phil's father was an atheist, and Phil considered himself an atheist as well. Both his parents were politically liberal and part of the socialist movement in Brooklyn in the 1950s.

The shock to the family over her extreme conversion was traumatic. As we were planning our wedding, Phil told me, "I don't think my sister is going to come. She's consulting with a number of rabbis on what to do."

"That's crazy. How could your sister not come to the wedding? It makes no sense," I said.

I just assumed the situation had gotten blown out of proportion. I never imagined she wouldn't be there. Phil was a devoted brother. He had been her rock before she became Hasidic, the person she turned to whenever she needed help with the apartment or to look after her two children. What reason could she have for not attending our wedding? We had recently gone to her Hasidic wedding, following the sect's tradition of men and women celebrating in separate rooms.

When she ultimately made her decision, the news was crushing: She would not attend our wedding. The rabbi had decreed that she could not acknowledge the indecent act her brother was committing by marrying someone who wasn't Jewish.

The rifts this created in the family as years passed were irreparable. Our children were not to be recognized as her children's cousins because they were not born of a Jewish mother. The family configuration was seismically altered along the fault lines of religious doctrine for decades to come.

Phil and I knew that any children we had would not go through any religious training: Catholic, Jewish, or otherwise. Religion was a creator of insurmountable differences driving people apart in the name of God. Its hardline, holier-than-thou beliefs would segregate anyone not held within its own narrow creed.

The supreme power in any religion always appeared to be male. As in every other aspect of life, men held the power. Your father brings home a good paycheck. Forgive me, Father, for I have sinned. Lord, I am not worthy to receive you. Male dominated paradigms created a hierarchy of power where one sat above and one sat below. The one above held the power over the one beneath them. I never imagined any other power structure than the traditional male-female hierarchy existed until many, many years later.

These cultural norms are downloaded into our being like software until the collective beliefs they add up to become our reality. The multidimensional programming system our choices and actions are based on—conditioned by education, religion, and family—has held the masculine principles in higher value for centuries, molding our mindsets and shaping our souls. Along with the dominance of this patriarchal paradigm has come the suppression of feminine principles, creating the imbalance of power we see in the world around us and reflected in the world within.

What is required now is a deconditioning to allow the feminine qualities of surrender and receptivity to blossom. In a masculine paradigm, control is the method for creation. We believe that in order to create we must be in control. The feeling that we must always control our circumstances, partners, feelings, and the flow of life itself is a fight against the pulse of our being, which exists in a state of fluidity.

Trying to "do" something in order to be in flow is an inherent contradiction, for the very essence of flow is "non-doing." Only a deconstruction of our age-old social and cultural conditioning can restore the balance of being and doing, of the masculine and feminine within us.

Start simple. Hold the intention to be in balance within you and around you, an intention to walk in a balanced way, for your heart and your mind to be in balance, for all beings to live in right relationship with Nature.

In 2007, the Dalai Lama was on the stage and I was in the audience at Radio City Music Hall in New York. It felt like an incredible privilege to be seeing him in person. In his common sense way, the Dalai Lama likened the intention of Buddhahood to making dinner.

Our intention to make the meal leads us to set the table and prepare the food, but that energy no longer drives our intent once the meal is complete. In the same way, holding the intention of Buddhahood's enlightenment will carry energy until the awakened state is achieved. Even if we do not see the intention come to fruition in our lifetime, its energy will continue on.

It is our intention that begins to carve the way for balance and harmony—between heart and mind, masculine and feminine, right thought and right action. This is the doing in the being. Let your intention be your guiding star. Then follow it: Listen, stay alert, be receptive, and be mindful.

CHAPTER EIGHT

The Road to Motherhood

MY ROAD TO MOTHERHOOD WAS fraught with struggle. A few years after Phil and I married, we were ready to start a family. It seemed like the natural next step in life. You have a career. You get married. You buy a home. You have children.

I stopped taking the pill but didn't get pregnant right away. Instead, I started taking my temperature to find my most fertile time of the month. Sex became a chore as it began revolving around when the basal body thermometer told me I was ovulating. After six months or more of trying, I missed a period. I took a pregnancy test, peed on the stick, and felt thrilled that the result was positive—at least until the nausea settled in. I was sick not just in the morning but all day long. Phil and I decided to wait until the first trimester had passed before telling our friends and family. My hope was that I would be feeling better by then, and the highest risks of pregnancy would be behind us.

At some point, the nausea lifted, leaving me with more energy. The worst symptoms of pregnancy seemed to be over. I was elated. At the twelfth week, we began to let people know we were expecting. The first reaction was, "Wow, you don't even look pregnant!"

"Yeah," I said. "I don't even feel pregnant!" Given how ill I had been, it was an enormous relief not to feel nauseous all the time. Then, two weeks after sharing the news that I was pregnant, I had a miscarriage.

Cramps woke me in the middle of the night. At first, it felt as if

I was getting my period. I had no other point of reference for what I was feeling. The cramps quickly became more rhythmic. I had an overwhelming urge to be on the toilet. I quietly got out of bed without waking Phil, went into the bathroom, and locked the door. The cramps were becoming stronger and closer together.

It wasn't long before it felt like the insides of my body were being emptied into the toilet. I began hemorrhaging. I had never seen so much blood. The cramps kept coming. I had no control over my body. I was hurled into survival mode trying to ride the pain, shock, and sheer horror of what was happening. I had no understanding of what was occurring, but it did not feel safe. I have no idea how much time passed, but eventually, the cramping and bleeding stopped. I flushed everything that had left my body down the toilet. Somehow, I thought I was still pregnant, that what had just happened was some kind of freak phenomenon of pregnancy. I couldn't let myself believe that what just occurred was the end of my pregnancy.

I never called for Phil who was still sleeping in the bedroom. For reasons I can't explain, I felt full of shame. My body had gone out of control.

Sitting behind a locked door in this terrifying uncertainty with blood pouring out of my body, I wanted privacy. I don't know if this is a natural response to bleeding out the contents of your uterus into the toilet. I never spoke to anyone about the details of what had happened or ever knew any other woman who miscarried. Perhaps it was the shattered hope I was afraid to face that kept me from calling out, even to a husband as dependable as Phil.

I went back to bed, unable to sleep. Eyes wide in terror, I stared at the ceiling. As the morning light poured in the windows, Phil woke up. I told him I'd had some bleeding during the night and was going to check in with my midwife. He didn't seem alarmed, but I hadn't given him any reason to be. I couldn't let myself believe what had happened during the night was alarming in any way.

When I called, the midwife said I needed to see her, and she confirmed my deepest fears. The pregnancy had actually been lost weeks earlier when the nausea vanished, she said. But for some reason, it had taken another four weeks, the length of a menstrual cycle, before my body would expel its contents. I was emotionally devastated and physically exhausted. I had pumped every ounce of adrenaline into my body to endure the unbearable waves that rocked my body the night before. Two weeks earlier, I'd been overjoyed to be sharing the news of my pregnancy. Now, I stood empty and ashamed. There had to be something wrong with me. I must have caused this to happen. I didn't know how I would ever face my family and friends to tell them I wasn't pregnant anymore.

The midwife said I would need a D&C to make sure my uterus was completely empty. I couldn't imagine anything was left inside, but as I was prepared for the procedure in her office, I realized immediately this was not the first time this was happening. The D&C was exactly what was done when I'd had an abortion fifteen years earlier for an accidental pregnancy that was shrouded in secrecy. I had thought an abortion was some stand-alone procedure used only to terminate a pregnancy. It never occurred to me that the same method would be used to ensure my health after a miscarriage.

Recovering physically took time, and I don't know how well I recovered emotionally. For months, the same dream startled me awake: Embedded in a wall in my home is a safe deposit box, its contents secured under lock and key. Inside are sparkling jewels and expensive treasures. I go to the box and unlock it. As I open the door, I see that it is empty. The treasures have been stolen. I stare in horror into the dark, empty hole in the wall. Frozen in fear, I cry inconsolable tears.

Three or four months must have passed before I started taking my temperature again and tracking my ovulation. When my period arrived each month, it felt like another miscarriage. It was a brutal reminder of the loss and further evidence I was not pregnant anymore. I was losing hope of ever becoming a mother. Everyone I knew was pregnant or having babies. Why was it so simple for them and so hard for me?

I was eventually told I had secondary infertility. The options were limited. Expensive fertility treatments involving test tube babies and implanted fetuses were financially out of reach. Medications to stimulate my hormones to ovulate felt like a risk to my health. Neither option seemed viable. Phil and I decided to start our family by adopting a baby. We had talked about adopting a child but thought we would have a biological child first. Life did not go as we planned. Parenthood began by adopting our first daughter.

Adoption felt safe. When you adopt a baby, they have already been born. Private open adoptions were becoming increasingly common in the U.S., structured to provide financial support during pregnancy for the mother who would then surrender her baby at birth. I was terrified the birthmother would change her mind. I could never bear the loss. We decided the risk was less if we looked internationally, and found that South Korea had a longstanding, streamlined system in place. Although we knew nothing of Korean culture, I had always felt an affinity with Eastern philosophies. In later years, as our daughter grew up, I tried to learn her native language and traditions and to help her know her heritage but there was no denying she would be assimilated into Western culture.

We eventually met with a social worker from Love the Children who worked with an adoption agency in South Korea. The process Phil and I went through was extensive, involving questions on everything from finances to parenting style. Three months after our application was approved, we were matched with our daughter, Ye Jin. The first thing we received was a 4x6 photo of her at two months old. She was zipped up in a pink onesie lying on a fluffy white blanket looking at us with jet black eyes. My heart broke open in love. I carried that photograph with me everywhere. I ached to hold her.

Waiting was the hardest part. It would be four months before she arrived. Our daughter would spend that time living with a foster mother in South Korea until the paperwork was in place that would allow her to leave. While we waited, we moved out of our apartment in Queens and bought a three-bedroom Colonial on a dead end street in the quaint village of Sea Cliff on the north shore of Long Island. Being there felt like a step back into simpler times. Old Victorian homes overlook Long Island Sound. Maple trees line streets free of sidewalks. Small parks and playgrounds are scattered through the mile-square village. The elementary school is the heartbeat of the community. We were surrounded by bustling suburbs while still less than thirty miles from Manhattan.

As I look back at my parenting style, it could have been lifted straight out of Mothering magazine, which I devoured every month. Although no longer in print, it called itself "the magazine of natural family living." My daughters wore cloth diapers, ate baby food made from scratch, and played with toys made of wood.

I kept busy by setting up her nursery as we waited for our daughter to come home. I found an exhilarating idea in a booklet called Breastfeeding Your Adopted Baby. Following its instructions, I bought a breast pump and sat with it attached to my breast while rocking in the glider in her nursery. I was full of hope that I would be nursing her once she arrived. Months of pumping never produced more than a drop of milk, which would never sustain her. Nevertheless, trying to squeeze milk from my breasts may have helped give my body some physical sense of preparing for my baby without actually going through a pregnancy.

The moment every family waits for with an international adoption is the day you pick up your baby at the airport. Months passed without a word until finally, our social worker called. Our daughter had arrived at Kennedy Airport, though no one had told us she was coming. Six babies for adoption were on the flight, escorted by South Koreans traveling to the U.S. A representative of the adoption agency, Love the Children, had called our social worker from the airport to find out why our daughter's parents weren't there. We must have seemed completely irresponsible.

We never learned the reason why we were never called. Instead, the social worker took our baby to her own home, where we met our daughter. It was there that I held her for the first time. She was six months old, with a big belly, full, round cheeks, and the tiniest bit of black fuzz covering her head. She had been born six weeks premature but seemed extremely healthy, more interested in putting everything in her mouth than she was in us. After painfully waiting for what had felt like an eternity to hold my daughter in my arms, the moment was surreal. I was a mother. I couldn't get enough of touching her and smelling her and holding her close. I held her in my lap in the backseat of our car as we drove home. I couldn't bear to part with her, even if it was to put her in the car seat.

We named our daughter Sarabeth after Phil's grandmother Sara along with part of my middle name Elizabeth. She was a good sleeper but took about a week to adjust to a time zone where her day was our night. I will never know how long other adjustments may have taken as her very young life had already been met with so much separation: from a birth mother, from a culture, from the smells and sounds of the country into which she was born. These things would take a lifetime to repair for her, but in that moment, the one I had waited so long for, I became a mother. Sarabeth was the most precious being I had ever met.

Then, three months later, came the biggest surprise: I found out I was pregnant. Being a new mother to Sarabeth was all-consuming. My first thoughts were: "I can barely manage one baby. How will I ever handle two?"

All my difficulties getting pregnant had left me feeling pretty infertile, and we had no plans for another baby anytime soon. After my miscarriage, I could see how afraid I was of losing another baby. Perhaps hormones or IVF would have helped me get pregnant again, but it was fear more than anything else, that prevented me from conceiving a child. Now Sarabeth was here. I was a mother. The fear of losing a baby was no longer my reality. Once my body felt safe to carry a baby is when I got pregnant, without a basal body thermometer or an ovulation calendar.

When my second daughter was finally ready to be born, labor lasted two days. The initial cramps were reminiscent of my miscarriage, but those cramps never reached the fierce force that is needed to push a baby out of your body. Twenty-four hours after my labor started, I thought for sure my baby was ready to be born. I called my midwife, and she had me come in for a quick office visit. Looking back on that conversation, I now know she could tell from the tone of my voice that I was nowhere near ready to give birth. She appeased me by having me come in for a quick check of my cervix.

I was dilated one centimeter—when I needed to be ten. I had no idea how I could possibly endure labor for much longer. The midwife called it prodromal labor, like trying to start your car when the engine won't turn over. She told me, "Go home. Take a warm bath and have a glass of wine."

I took her advice, and shortly after stepping out of the tub, my water broke. The labor catapulted into another dimension. The force moving through my body was no longer something I could will into submission. It took over my body and gave me no choice but to surrender to the primordial wisdom that knows how to birth a baby. It was as if I had tapped into the ancient lineage of women who have been giving birth since the beginning of time. The energy of every woman who had ever been in labor was with me. My body was a vessel through which a venerable intelligence moved through and brought my baby safely into the world.

Danielle was born less than two hours after I arrived at the hospital. Once I surrendered to the ferocity of the force moving through me, my labor progressed rapidly. I gave birth to a healthy seven-pound, nine-ounce girl on the morning of September 12, 1994, a year after Sarabeth's arrival from South Korea. It was hard to believe that the baby who had been squirming inside me was now on the other side. Despite my arduous labor, I was filled with incredible wonder at the miracle that had just occurred. Danielle's arrival was the most sacred experience of my life.

The utter helplessness of a newborn was a new experience for me. Sarabeth had arrived at six months old, sturdy enough to sit upright with some control over her body. Danielle was so tiny and helpless in comparison. Although I had been a mother for a year, having a newborn was strange and unfamiliar. I started nursing Danielle right away. Although my breasts had gotten larger during pregnancy, I was unprepared for the engorgement once my milk came in. If I had pumped for Sarabeth non-stop for a year, I couldn't produce the amount of milk that filled my breasts after Danielle was born.

Rocking in that glider nursing Danielle gave me some of the most beloved memories of those early years—and unexpectedly helped my dream of nursing Sarabeth also come true. At eighteen months old, she was curious watching her sister at my breast, so I cradled Sarabeth in my arms and brought her there as well. To my astonishment, she started sucking right away. Nursing Sarabeth was not to meet any nutritional needs, but the bond created a deeper attachment for us both.

In all these things that I went through—my miscarriage, pregnancy, labor, and delivery—I felt the sovereign power and ancient wisdom of my female body deep in my bones. Yet somehow our culture has taught many women to condemn—even to loathe—our bodies, to judge them based on wrinkles and folds, curves and cellulite. The reality is that the female body is the highest manifestation of Divine Creation on our planet, for she carries the womb, the vessel from which life springs forth. Even man emerges from the body of a woman.

This is something to realize about your body, to know deeply. How does your body make you feel? Do you criticize or judge it? Being truly aware that you have been given a temple can help you develop a more loving relationship with your body just as it is.

Do you know anyone who would work twenty-four hours a day, seven days a week, never taking a break and never receiving a thank you for their tireless efforts? This is your body. Think of all the jobs it does day in and day out. Your heart hasn't stopped pumping since your time in the womb. Your lungs are always giving you the oxygen that you need for survival. Like an ever-running engine, your digestive system converts what you eat into the fuel whose energy lets you function. The jobs your body is constantly doing to sustain your life are endless.

Bring a sense of wonder to your body. Treat it with appreciation to help heal and restore right relationship, what the shamans call ayni, between you and your body. Holding your body sacred helps brings the sacred to everything in your life. Thank your body for the living, breathing miracle that it is. Ask what it needs to feel nourished and supported. Listen to its inner wisdom. What can you do to demonstrate your appreciation for your body and honor its needs? Does it need more air, more hydration, more or less of something in its diet? Listen to your body with an attitude of gratitude. We would have a far different—and far better—world if every woman honored her body as the sacred temple that it is, appreciating rather than criticizing what is inside her.

CHAPTER NINE

The Sovereign Right to Control Our Body

GIVEN MY PREVIOUS CHALLENGES WITH infertility three years earlier, it should have been a joyous occasion to learn that I was pregnant again. Instead, with Danielle still nursing, an oppressive weight descended, a weight that felt impossible to crawl out from under. The demands of mothering two little ones were overwhelming. The thought of a third felt like a crushing responsibility I could not carry.

Soon after I learned I was pregnant, my grandfather died. He was one of the gentlest souls on the planet, loved by everyone, but babies loved him most of all. Just sitting on his lap could settle any of his grandchildren's fussing. My grandfather was proud to be a subway conductor for the New York City Transit Authority. In those days before electrification, subway cars connecting Manhattan to other boroughs through underground tunnels and elevated tracks were fueled by coal. He never smoked a day in his life, but the smoke of burning coal was enough to give him lung cancer. He loved to show off the scar that wrapped around his chest after one of his lungs was removed, proving that he had indeed beat cancer. But not forever. Eventually, it would return and spread to his liver. My grandfather died peacefully in his home.

As much as I loved my grandfather. he was not someone I would seek counsel from about an unwanted pregnancy. Now that he was gone, with my heart broken open in grief for him, it felt safe to seek his guidance and ask for a sign. He felt like a guardian angel watching over me with his gentle loving soul. At the funeral, his daughter Lilyan read from the Unity Church's Daily Word:

> *Right at this moment, children are being born, and fresh new life is coming into the world. So we say: God bless you, children, and welcome. Welcome to a world we cherish, live in, and share with you and the whole family of God.*

I thought for sure my grandfather was speaking to me through those words. The message seemed clear: Keep the baby. Holding the anguish of my unplanned pregnancy, I wept for my grandfather and for the burden I felt I was carrying. Only Phil, who supported whatever decision I made, knew of the pregnancy. Lilyan read on.

> *And there is rebirth going on also, for some of us are discovering or rediscovering our true identity. As magnificently as our physical bodies are designed, we are even greater than what we appear to be. At the core of the human form, we are spiritual beings, created in the image of God. We are the children of the Creator. The rebirth we go through is a fantastic discovery of our own spirituality.*

"There is a rebirth going on. Some of us are discovering our true identity."

I recognized those words as a choice, my choice. I was carrying a life I had not planned for. I was no longer taking the pill since I was still nursing Danielle. Sex was rare in our marriage because of the exhausting demands of work and parenting. I felt utterly irresponsible about getting pregnant in the first place. There were no more needs left in me to sacrifice. The rebirth that was going on was the discovery of my own true identity.

This was not the first time I was contemplating the end of a pregnancy. I was nineteen, living at home and attending a community college. All I remember was his first name.

Mark.

I met him one night at a bar on Long Island. He was a few years older than me, but I remembered him from high school. We'd never spoken or hung out together, yet we recognized each other in some vaguely familiar way. We ended up talking and drinking and ultimately left the bar together, with me following him home in my car. We had sex in his bedroom, and I left before his family woke up.

I'd never kept very good track of my period. I had never heard of the word "ovulation" and had no understanding of fertility. Back then, contraceptive foam and a condom were the ways you kept from getting pregnant. I had neither. Six weeks or more must have passed before I realized I hadn't gotten my period in a while. At-home pregnancy tests had just become available a year earlier.

Those early tests were not the simple pee-on-a-stick-and-find-out-in-a-few-moments kind. The first home pregnancy tests were more like chemistry kits involving compounds and urine and test tubes and waiting hours to find out if you were pregnant. I told no one what I feared might be true. I bought the kit in a drugstore a few towns away to make sure no one I knew would see, and smuggled it into the bathroom where I locked the door to pee in a cup. The urine had to be mixed with some solution that went into a test tube that sat above an angled mirror. A red ring appeared hours later if you were pregnant. I hid the test in my bedroom closet while I waited to see if the ring appeared.

It did. I was pregnant. I don't remember my initial reaction, but I do remember the fantasies that followed. Having a baby felt like I would finally have someone to love me. That seemed to be the reason a baby comes into the world: to love the one who brought it there. That was the delusion that fed my initial desires to keep the baby—with no thoughts that were based in reality. How could I afford a baby or raise one? What would be the impact on my life, my family's life, my future? There was no rational thinking about any of these questions. I just wanted someone to love me. That seemed to be what a baby would bring to my life.

I told no one other than my best friend, Tammy, who said I had to tell Mark. She was also the one who told me I couldn't possibly have the baby: "What are you thinking? How are you going to raise a baby? What are you, crazy?" She was the dark dose of reality killing my dream for love.

Weeks passed before I saw Mark again. I didn't have his phone number. The only way to let him know I was pregnant was to drive back to his home. Drunk. Just like I did the first time. I entered his home late at night through an unlocked back door. Everyone was sleeping. I walked in as quietly as I could and went upstairs to the bedroom we had sex in. He was scared to death when I walked into his room in the middle of the night.

He quickly ushered me out of the house. We sat in my car. He was disheveled and groggy as I told him, "I'm pregnant."

"You're kidding me. How do you know it's mine?" he argued. There was no one else I'd had sex with, either before or after him. I knew he was the reason I was pregnant, whether he wanted to believe me or not.

"I'm seeing someone else," he said. He didn't really care what I did as far as the pregnancy was concerned, but he definitely had no interest in having a baby and wanted nothing to do with raising one if I decided to keep it. There was no offer of help, no offer of money. He opened the car door, stepped out, and slammed it shut. That was the last time I saw Mark. He was able to walk away from any responsibility. His life could go on. Just like that. I never felt more utterly alone.

The alcohol that had given me the courage to face Mark also numbed me to the rage I felt. I couldn't just slam the door and rid myself of this pregnancy. My body did not give me that kind of freedom. Unless I did something, my life would be irrevocably altered in ways that were beyond my limited comprehension at the time. The dark dose of reality was setting in.

It is only through the lens of time that I see how fortunate I was to be a young woman living on Long Island in 1979. The landmark Roe v. Wade decision had legalized abortions in the U.S. a few years earlier. I lived near a Bill Baird abortion clinic that had recently opened in Suffolk County. Baird's crusade for reproductive rights began in 1963 when he witnessed a woman bleed to death in the halls of Harlem Hospital after trying to give herself an abortion with a coat hanger. Before abortion was legal, desperate women resorted to sticking metal coat hangers up their vagina to end an unwanted pregnancy, with sometimes fatal consequences.

Baird was the clinical director of a birth control company and was first arrested in 1967 for giving spermicidal foam to a nineteen year student on the campus of Boston University. The arrest fueled his activism which ultimately took him to the U.S. Supreme Court where the decision was made to allow unmarried people the same right to birth control as those who were married.

I did not know any of this as I entered the Bill Baird Clinic in Hempstead, thirty minutes from home. A small group of people were camped outside. Some had signs with pictures of babies and fetuses in the womb. I was too afraid to look at any of them, but I could hear them yelling.

"Your baby wants to live."

"It's not too late to change your mind."

"Think about the baby you are killing."

"Baby killer!" they called out.

I focused straight ahead on the building entrance in front of me. In the sparse, sterile waiting room, I filled out forms and handed over $200 in cash, most of the money in my savings account.

I had built up those funds as often as I could, adding money from working as a babysitter starting when I was eleven. I moved up to a cashier at a local grocery store and was now working as a waitress. Seeing those numbers add up in my little savings account booklet gave me a feeling of security. I could take care of myself. Now I was destroying that security to pay for a reckless night with expensive consequences that were mine alone to bear. I felt nauseous and ashamed and terrified of what was about to happen.

I waited in the gown I'd been given in a small room with a metal table and a large machine next to it. A doctor came in. I assume he gave some explanation of what was to happen, but I was too petrified to remember anything at all. I lay back with my feet in the stirrups and my legs apart. A speculum entered my vagina and the vacuum machine started to whir. My insides began tearing away from my body.

The whirring machine felt like it was punishing me for every flagrant, irresponsible, reckless, and deranged thought or deed I'd ever committed. There was sharp, sharp cramping, more pain than I had ever felt in my life. I endured the torture by barely breathing, holding it all in until the whirring stopped and it was over. I was given a number of heavy sanitary napkins and left alone to get dressed. I drove myself home. No one other than my best friend Tammy and the guy named Mark ever knew I was pregnant.

I had an abortion. I had a miscarriage. I was diagnosed with secondary infertility. I adopted a daughter. I gave birth to a daughter. I was nearing the end of my reproductive life cycle and was back where I had started it: contemplating an abortion.

To others, I appeared to be a happy wife and mother. My debilitating unhappiness was visible only to me. I was supposed to be happy, and the fact that I was not only deepened my self-loathing. I had bought into the notion that having a good provider as a husband, a home in the suburbs, and lovely children would make me happy. Even though the happily-ever-after dream may not have been based in reality, clinging to it as an ideal is what created my life in the first place. You got married, you bought a house, you had kids, and all those things would make me as happy as the perfect homemakers who solved every family problem each week in the TV episodes I believed in.

There had been seven channels on television when I was growing up. Most of America watched the same thing at the same time:

"The Donna Reed Show," "Father Knows Best," and "Leave It to Beaver." The images that programmed us were downloaded into my psyche. Women were always stay-at-home moms. For my mother, even her jobs outside the home were rooted in domestic work. She was a lunch lady at our school cafeteria when we were growing up and started cleaning houses after she and my dad moved to Florida. I am proud of my mother. In no way do I diminish her work or that of other women, which we have collectively undervalued in our culture. But the disparity between how I saw women both in my home and on TV as I was growing up and the unhappiness in my own life was so painful that the only conclusion I could draw was that something must be wrong with me.

On the night this hit me hardest, Danielle woke up crying in the middle of the night. She had just turned two. It would be another two years before she consistently slept through the night. I often felt as if I was sleep walking through my life. As I went into her bedroom to console her, Sarabeth, who was now three and a half and normally slept through the night, started crying as well. Having to console them both in the middle of the night was unusual.

Getting up with my daughters in the middle of the night was my job since I was still nursing Danielle, even though I'd returned to work part time. I loved my daughters more than anything I had ever loved. I would have given my life for them. but this particular night brought a weighty suffering to light. Phil was running his private physical therapy practice full time, and even though we were both working, the money we made barely covered our expenses each month.

And even worse, I was exhausted all the time. That night, holding two crying babies and knowing another was growing inside me left me sobbing inconsolably in a heap on my daughter's bedroom floor. The crushing weight of the pregnancy was more than I could bear. Many women have more than two children, including my own mother who had five. How weak could I be that I couldn't handle one more? I felt selfish, as if I was not doing enough, and yet deeply ashamed of being so inadequate as a mother. The emotional and mental torment of that night took its toll. I could not imagine my life with another person in the world to take care of, either financially or emotionally.

I decided to end the pregnancy. This time, the decision was not viewed through the drunken delusions of a teenager but as a woman who knew full well the consequences of my action. It was the most tortured decision I ever made. I couldn't imagine life without either of my daughters, yet I was willing to forsake the life growing inside me. I could only describe it as a matter of survival—my own.

Phil supported my decision. The abortion seemed to be a time stamp that marked the slow and spiraling dissolution of our marriage. Maybe it was all the personal emotion I was caught up in while also having to deal with Phil's feelings, which left our home life in a heightened state of tension. It would be a few more years before I could find the courage to speak the words that would obliterate my life as I knew it.

As I write this, Roe v. Wade has been overturned. I heard the news driving to my first home therapy visit on the morning of June 24, 2022. Although there had been hints it would happen, I still thought it was impossible. I felt as if some new horror was holding me down. Alone in my car, I screamed. A primal scream that felt as if it reached back in time to every woman who has ever been held down and held back at the hands of a patriarch who must dominate in order to control. Although the contrasts could not have been more stark between the two choices I made to end an unwanted pregnancy, being unable to make that choice at all had never occurred to me. At the most basic level, there is no act that can disempower a woman more completely than to take away her right to control her own body.

The idea that women can be victimized in this way—the belief among men that they somehow have the inherent power to do this—is a throwback to the misaligned myth of Eve as the seductive temptress leading Adam to the original sin of eating the forbidden fruit. Over all the centuries, men have expended massive amounts of energy to suppress the creativity and wisdom of the feminine. This is what our sacred role as the carriers of life represents. If you have been gifted with a female body, your reproductive life cycle may or may not include giving birth. Regardless, you can look at your life through the lens of the sacred mystery of your womb: What has brought you the deepest joy? What has caused your greatest suffering? Did you want to have children but couldn't? Perhaps you didn't want children but have felt the pressure of a society that feels giving birth is the role of a woman, especially one who is married. You may have birthed things other than children in your life. The womb is the source of your sacred feminine wisdom. Connect with it. Give yourself ten minutes—without stopping—and write a letter that starts, Dear Womb. Hear the guidance it can give you.

CHAPTER TEN

We Have to Talk

IT TOOK ONE CONVERSATION FOR my marriage to suddenly end. There was no dramatic event that led to its downfall. The erosion was more like an insidious weight that encapsulated my heart, dulling my ability to invest emotion into the life I was living. I was frozen in a complex paradox. I was terrified to end the marriage while at the same time terrified to remain in a marriage that by any measure was considered a success.

Phil was a hardworking husband devoted to our two daughters. He provided for our family as the owner of a private physical therapy practice. We had a mortgage on an old Colonial on a dead-end street in a charming Long Island village. In summer, kids played on the block until the streetlights came on. We had a front porch, a finished basement, and a small yard. I walked our daughters to their elementary school in the morning and picked them up in the afternoon, in one of the best school districts in the state. Life was picture perfect. Why was I so unhappy? How could I feel trapped in such an idyllic life? Why couldn't I just be grateful for everything I had? As I lived my days plagued by paralyzing fear, perpetual self-doubt, and a deep self-loathing, enlightenment dropped itself into a jar of coins.

During our marriage, Phil and I collected loose change in an old glass water cooler. It stood three feet high and sat in the corner on a landing at the base of the stairs. The first time I ever rolled up the change that had dropped into that jar, we had nearly $700 in assorted paper coin wrappers to take to the bank. After that windfall, I became diligent about saving coins. One day, as I threw the change from my pocket into the glass water cooler, my wedding band accidentally landed in there too. It had been in a pocket where I often put it while working with patients as a physical therapist.

The jar was heavy enough on its own. The weight of the coins inside made it even more cumbersome to manage. To get coins out of the jar, you had to turn it on its side with the back end lifted up so they would slide out the narrow neck. The coins always jammed as they tried to pass through the tiny opening. It took a lot of unwieldy maneuvering of the heavy glass jar to get anything to come out. Given the time it would take to wrangle my ring from the jar of coins, I left it in there. I had dinner to make and daughters to tend to after a day of work.

Days passed before Phil asked, "Why aren't you wearing your wedding band?" I told him about how it had landed in the money jar. When he realized I hadn't tried to get it out, he was furious. I could see the jar sitting on the landing from where we stood in the living room. As I faced my raging husband with my wedding band stuck in the jar of money, I was seized by the light of truth. I felt trapped in my marriage because of the money. Any thoughts of leaving my marriage because of our deep emotional disconnect always boiled down to finances. Our money was just about covering the cost of one household. The expense of two was out of the question. I was right where my eight-year-old self had vowed never to be: powerless and dependent on a man for money. My life had circled back to the same predicament my mother had found herself in. The moment of enlightenment that came from that jar of money could not be unseen. My throat was perpetually clenched for fear I might say something that would end the marriage, yet the thought of staying married felt like an endless trap I could not escape from. I was stuck, just like my wedding band in that jar of money.

There had to be something wrong with me. Everyone loved Phil. He was the heart of a large circle of childhood friends from Brooklyn. Although most of his friends had left the borough after marrying, we all headed to the Jersey Shore every summer for a beach vacation. We rented a house large enough for eight adults and sixteen kids. Phil volunteered his time to athletes with disabilites. He ran marathons with amputees. He traveled to the Paralympic games over the years, all without any financial reimbursement. How could I walk away from someone as beloved as Phil?

Though we stayed together, our relationship remained fragile. I didn't have the courage to talk to him about my feelings, and my body could not keep faking love and desire. Sex became a barter to keep the peace. I knew that once we had sex, there would be a few days in which I wouldn't have to do it again. I remember the night we were married at the Boathouse in Central Park. It was an ecstatic celebration. My sister-in-law had gotten us a room at the Hyatt hotel in Manhattan where she worked. It saved us the trip of heading back to Brooklyn that night. When we got back to the hotel, I was exhausted. Knowing all the money we had spent on our wedding, coupled with my own scarcity beliefs, all I wanted to do with whatever energy I had left was open our wedding envelopes. Phil wanted sex. I couldn't say no on our wedding night. It felt like an obligation, like something I had to do to keep peace even from the very beginning. Finally, years later, the "bartering" over sex became too much. I stopped altogether, hoping that would drive him away.

Phil was highly emotional. I often thought he had enough emotion for the two of us in our marriage. He expressed himself emotionally much more than I did. My emotional default pattern was to shut down. The only time I remember expressing any rage was when we were having sex. I would often feel an overwhelming urge to bite him, not out of passion but from a desire to rip him apart. A primal rage that wanted to hurt him as much as I was hurting. I had to hold myself back from truly harming him.

All this went on without his knowing how much anger I felt during sex. After we stopped, despite the absence of sex, the last thing Phil wanted was for our marriage to end. He had lived through two divorces in his family: his mother and father's and then the end of his father's second marriage. It was a pain he did not want to inflict on his own children. No one in my family had ever been divorced. Despite my dad's drinking, my parents stayed together until the end. I never imagined anyone in my family would understand why I would want a divorce. My family loved Phil. We tried therapy for a short time, but by then, the marriage seemed beyond repair, even though it lingered on for another year.

Around this time, I was taking the Phoenix Rising yoga therapy training in Massachusetts. We were assigned a mentor who remained in communication with us between our weekend trainings. I can remember falling in love with her. The desire to be with her was like something I had never felt before, certainly nothing I had ever felt with Phil. Was that what love is? Is that what married people are supposed to feel? The feelings seemed to rise from exposing myself to someone and being met with validation and affirmation rather than judgment and criticism. I felt listened to and heard in a way I had never experienced before. The feelings were not about my sexual preference since she was a woman but rather showed me the absence of love in my relationship with my husband. The feelings did not create an affair but caused a further disintegration of the investment in my marriage.

I was afraid to end it but also afraid of staying married. Trying to ease the painful and palpable tensions between us, Phil would approach me and say, "We have to talk." It was never really "we" talking so much as Phil venting his fears and frustrations. He would let off steam and then nothing would change. My throat was choked with fear. I have never been adept at expressing myself emotionally. I learned to manage emotions by manufacturing feelings that were expected rather than expressing whatever feelings may have been true. The way for me to get through our "We have to talk sessions" was to dodge the emotional landmines and not make him more angry. One wrong look could set the stage for arguments recycled on endless loops, never finding resolution.

I existed in my marriage by numbing myself to the tensions between us. I could never find the words to say what I felt because I was afraid that my words would end the marriage. I was afraid of the finances. I was afraid of the effect on our daughters. I was afraid of how we would survive. I was afraid of how the framework of our family could possibly be rearranged in a way that would not cause harm. Ultimately, I was frozen in fear. The only escape route seemed to be divorce, although it took six long years for that to become reality.

The night before our final "we have to talk" conversation, I had attended a shamanic trance dance. Trance dancing had become an emotional outlet that probably kept me from losing my mind altogether. During the dance we were blindfolded while moving our bodies to the rhythmic beats of live drumming.

The blindfold eliminated any inhibitions since we could not see each other during the dance allowing the power of movement to course freely through our bodies. Before the dance started, we stood in a ceremonial circle and selected a power animal from a deck of cards to guide us during the dance. Mine was Raven. Its medicine was Magic. The message sent through the dance was Trust.

In that dance, with my body moving as its own master, I had a visceral knowing that I must trust my heart as my truest voice, and be guided by the wisdom of the feelings within me. The next morning, as Phil and I sat at the top of the staircase to our finished attic where I practiced yoga each morning and our daughters played house with their wooden kitchen set, we had our final talk. I dropped my head. All I could say was, "My heart is not in this anymore." Phil responded, "I have to move out."

There was no dramatic incident. There was no illicit affair. There was no domestic abuse or violence. There was no rational reason I could come up with for ending our marriage. I could not keep investing my heart. I could not keep going through the motions of a picture-perfect life. I could not keep pretending I was happy. I could not keep having sex. I was worn out.

Once the truth spilled from my heart, I was terrified. My life as I knew it was being blown to pieces. I had no idea where those pieces would land or what it would take to pick up the fragmented shards and create something new. At the same time, the terror was intertwined with the most intense liberation I had ever felt. Images of "The Donna Reed Show" and "Father Knows Best" with pictures of the perfect homemakers wearing neatly tied aprons with never a hair out of place solving all the family problems in a single episode were literally flashing through my mind. Their perfection was the corrupted feminine that I was aspiring to; their images liberated from outdated archives and set free so they could no longer shape my identity from the shadows.

The picket fence around the idyllic home of my imagination blew up.

The perfect wife blew up.

The perfect family blew up.

I was scared to death.

And utterly free.

For too long, the fear of what might follow had kept me from moving on with my life. It was only through overcoming that fear that I could end my marriage and open the door to my future. To be safe, we must leave all that we know behind. To be secure means to release the bonds that have held our soul captive.

We do not want our beliefs threatened, for they are the bedrock of our safety. Belief systems are the lens through which we see the world around us. Yet true safety, true security, will not be found until we are stripped naked, until there is nothing left to be seen, until there is nowhere left to hide. Then, when those beliefs are no longer able to hold us back, we can see what the world truly opens us up to.

There were so many constructs I built my life on that only turned out to threaten what freedom could give me. They had to implode and collapse first. Many of our belief systems are rooted in fear and scarcity: fear of being alone, fear of the unknown, fear of not enough. Our fear is completely dedicated to keeping us safe from what our mind imagines might be harmful. Fear is much like an overprotective mother. It is acting in our best interest, keeping us safe and protected, but also limiting our growth and development. We become frozen.

What are you afraid of doing in your life right now? Are you avoiding communicating with someone because you fear they'll be angry? Is there an idea you're afraid to put forth because it might be rejected? Are you putting off ending a relationship for fear of being alone? Are you afraid to speak up for fear of humiliation? If you are living a life that fears to move forward, your body will know. And it will tell you. It might be with a tenseness, with a heaviness, with a pain, with a weakness. Be aware of where this happens—and then go there.

Whatever part of your body is receiving this message, be aware, and put your focus and attention there. Trying to push fear away or fight against it is doomed, for it will only fight back stronger and persist. What will help you release fear is kindness, compassion, and—above all else—love. Wherever it is hurting you, nurture that part of yourself; treat it as a child or a pet who is afraid. Place your hands there; it's where the fear lives. Love that fear, for it is no less sacred than your love. It is equally a part of you. Do not diminish or condemn your fear like some lower aspect of yourself. Don't treat it as if it's unworthy, for it is not. It is of you, and as such, it deserves your love and attention.

As you unearth parts of yourself that have been hidden in shadow, feelings, anxieties, or memories may come to light. You can reach out to them. For me, writing letters can deepen communication with aspects of myself that may be in hiding. You can start with, Dear Fear. Write for ten minutes—nonstop. A sacred discomfort may arise as you move past limitations into new and sometimes-uncomfortable territory. Above all else, be gentle with yourself.

CHAPTER ELEVEN

Beauty Corrupted

THREE DAYS AFTER MY FATHER died, I was on a plane to Peru. It had been about six years since my divorce, and my first time traveling there. I had been studying shamanic knowledge and practices for many years, and wanted to actually experience the teachings from their original source. Through the Four Winds Society, I had been learning shamanic ceremonies, rituals, soul retrievals, and Earth-based medicine practices of the shamans of the high Andes. A mentor from the Four Winds had organized the trip to travel and study with the shamans. It was a trip I had been dreaming of for years. Along with the two women who led the journey, a small group of six women and three men made up the group, including my younger sister, Kristine.

From New York, we flew to Lima and then Cusco, once the capitol of the Incan Empire, now a bustling city that is both cosmopolitan and ancient. Cobblestone streets lined with markets lead to central plazas where cathedrals with ornately carved doors soar three stories high to welcome weary souls. Our ultimate destination was the holy mountain of the Andes, Umantay.

We spent the first few days in 9,000-foot-high Cusco to acclimate to the altitude. I was grateful to have my sister with me. Our father had died a few days before we got on the plane. He had been sick with cancer for the past year and receiving hospice care for the last ten days at his home in Florida. Death had been imminent.

Kristine and I had talked about what might happen if he died while we were in Peru. Would we need to return home in the middle of our trip? Would anyone be able to reach us in the mountains with news that our father had died? It seemed better that he died before we left, but were we heartless to fly off on an adventure so soon afterward? To some degree, it eased our conscience to know that at least we were not missing his funeral. His body was cremated, and a family memorial service was planned for a month later in New York.

Each day in Peru was filled with activity, leaving little time to pause or contemplate my father's death. We rose early each morning for short excursions to nearby sacred sites, shared in ceremonies with the shamans we were traveling with and shopped the markets for handwoven textiles, ceremonial rattles, hand-made leather bags, and custom-made boots.

After a few days in busy Cusco, the day arrived to head to Umantay. At our hotel, a merchant in the lobby offered my sister and I alpaca wool ponchos to take to the mountain. He assured us they would keep us warm at the higher altitudes. He did not ask for money. If we liked them, we could buy them when we returned. No one I had ever known in the states did business this way. He seemed so trusting of us. My sister was given a beautiful cream-colored poncho. Mine was a very bright and bold turquoise. The poncho was big and heavy and draped below my knees. It had buttons down the front and a scarf around the neck. I loved that you did not have to pull the poncho over your head. You could just wrap it around your shoulders and button the front to close it.

To be swathed in such an audacious color felt awkwardly uncomfortable. I was born and raised in New York. Black was the dominant color of my wardrobe. The poncho made me stand out way too much. I didn't want to insult the merchant by trying to exchange it for another color when he wasn't even asking for money. One of the women leading the journey heard me say how uncomfortable I felt wearing such a bold color. "Stop trying to blend," she told me.

"When you stop yourself from standing out, it keeps you safe." She was right. I had taught myself to dim my light. The bright turquoise poncho made me feel way too dazzling. As awkward as it felt to be swathed in such a glaring color, I took it with me to the mountain. It was a bumbling step toward brilliance.

Heading for Umantay, we all piled into a minivan with much of our personal gear strapped on top. The paved highways turned to dirt roads as we climbed higher along hairpin turns up the rugged mountainside. With no guardrail in sight, we felt precariously close to falling off the edge at any moment. At some point, our van pulled off into a clearing where we joined with another van that had the rest of our group, then added a medicine woman, two medicine men, and a number of wranglers who carried what we needed to set up camp, including a kitchen tent and port-a-potty. It was quite a luxurious base camp for the remote mountains of Peru.

Eventually, the vans stopped and our trek began on foot. Each of us had a sleeping bag, clothing, and personal gear stuffed into our backpacks. The day was bright and clear, the air crisp. Climbing was slow because of the weight and altitude, somewhere between thirteen thousand and fourteen thousand feet. My lungs felt as if they were being pressured into places they'd never been before. I was feeling the effort with every step.

Along the way, we would stop to pray and leave offerings of coca leaves in apuchettas, the shrines we would build with small stones. Every prayer we placed between the stones was to say thank you—to Pachamama, our Earth Mother; to Inti Ti-Ti, Father Sun; to the ancestors and spirit allies guiding us safely along our journey. There was never a prayer asking for help in getting to the top of the mountain or any other destination. It was always to give thanks for how far we had come. Praying in this way opened my eyes to a new way of seeing. And offering gratitude for how far we had come opened my spirit to something far different from what praying had been before, always about asking for something or getting somewhere.

The air as we gained altitude seemed to have a clarity that brought all my senses to attention. Few people had walked these mountains where we now stood. I had never before felt the land pulsing beneath me. It was what the shamans called undomesticated, never cultivated. The land was wild and free with nothing built or paved to mar its topography, and it coursed through our veins as if to let us know that we too were alive.

I had never been at such high altitudes before. The low air pressure made my eyes puffy and swollen. It wasn't painful but made me feel hideously ugly. I felt so distorted I wanted to hide in shame and not be seen. The ugliness I felt became a barrier between myself and others.

Once we reached camp and began to settle in, I was ashamed to let anyone know how ugly I felt—or how vain I was. Doña Berna, one of the medicine women we were traveling with, placed wet coca leaves around my eyes to reduce the swelling, but they didn't help. I felt as if I was pretending with the others since I did not want to reveal how ugly I felt but my swollen face could not hide the obvious. I don't think anyone else cared how I looked, but for me, it was all-consuming. I felt the puffiness of my eyes and could see with my phone camera how hideously distorted I looked. I was repulsed by the grotesque reflection staring back at me.

In the deepest recesses of the feminine, my looks mattered. They were the measure of my worth as a woman. My appearance was what got a man to pay attention. It was a competition among women, since the most attractive woman is the one who wins. I was not consciously aware of all this on the mountain, as all of my energy was obsessing over how ugly I looked. I had come to believe that a woman's power was in her looks. I was not aware that the immense power of the Apus would soon reveal a truth I did not know existed.

After base camp was set up, our small group gathered in a circle sitting atop blankets on the ground. We were far, far above tree line surrounded by the majestic snow-capped peaks. An avalanche of snow tumbling down the mountain looked like a mystical waterfall.

Eagles and condors soared overhead in the purity of the clean, crisp air. My mentor, Elle, who was leading the journey, created a safe space in the circle with a prayer calling to the four directions. In the Andean cosmology, Serpent sits in the south. It is where we shed and release what no longer serves us. In the west is Jaguar, symbol of death and rebirth. In the north is Hummingbird, the direction of gifts and blessings. In the east is Eagle/Condor, the direction of new visions.

The circle was a time to sit and reflect and check in with each other after the arduous trek that took nearly all day. During the sharing circle, each person expressed gratitude for being on this journey, for being on the mountain surrounded by such beauty. Everyone seemed to be overflowing with gratitude and joy. But I was still consumed with how ugly I looked. I sat in fearful anticipation as the voices around the circle moved closer; soon all eyes would be on me. I wanted to bury myself so deep underground that I could not be seen. My mind struggled to think out what I should say.

Ultimately, it answered. I had not traveled all this way to sit on a holy mountain in Peru and spew lies about what I was feeling. I was surrounded by beauty, yet nothing within me had any access to it.

As the circle landed on me, my head dropped. I couldn't look anyone in the eye. I spoke of how ugly I felt. I spoke of how embarrassed I was about feeling so ugly. I spoke of how I wanted to feel grateful and feel the beauty all around me that everyone else was experiencing, but all I could see and all I could feel was my own ugliness. It was the only lens through which I could see the world. Somehow, the mountains had magnified my perception of how ugly I was. My body racked with sobs as I spoke.

As I sat near the top of the world, on a holy mountain in Peru, tears poured from my swollen eyes as the lies of the false prophets of beauty were laid before me. Time and again, for as long as I could remember, the false prophets of beauty had preached to me through advertisements, magazine covers, commercials, movies, TV ads. The sermon of these false prophets was what I believed. It was a belief system that left me feeling as if I was never enough—not much different from how the priests had left me feeling in church.

Wherever I looked, the message was the same. I am not pretty enough. I am not thin enough. I am not flawless enough. I am not young enough. I am not perfect enough. My stomach is not flat enough. My skin is not tight enough. My hair is not silky enough. Plain and simple, who I was, as I was, was never enough.

As much as I wanted to believe I had not fallen prey to marketers looking only for profit, I knew that their lies about beauty were woven deep into the fabric of my psyche. The bombardment of images had been scorched into my subconscious over all the decades of my life. Now I saw these images floating before my eyes. In that moment I was elevated from the tyranny the web of lies had brought upon me. Sitting in that circle, I was met with understanding and love and empathy. I no longer saw myself through the lens of ugliness with my value measured only by how I looked. I was able to authentically connect with my fellow travelers there in a way that felt real and—more important—felt beautiful.

Once our circle disbanded, Judy, the other woman leading the trip approached me and said, "Have I got a journey for you!" She had just finished her first trip to Peru solely for women to Awaken the Divine Feminine. I had no idea what that meant, but in that moment, a chastened voice shackled in the subterrain of my soul said "Yes".

There is a spiritual code of beauty learned from the shamans in Peru that is far different from how our Western world views beauty. We have learned to place a value judgment on beauty simply by what can be seen. There is also the feeling of beauty, which touches the sacred. It is the feeling that comes when we are watching the sun rise or delighting in the scent of a rose or holding a baby in our arms. We are reminded of our holiness by beauty. It is a spiritual way of being that has been corrupted and expressed in ways that are not in alignment with its sacred essence.

This corruption of beauty has been extremely destructive for women in many ways. It generates competition. It creates eating disorders. It sends messages that permeate our psyche and create a self-loathing that perpetuates itself in both the relationship with one's own body and the body's relationship with the planet we live on. This self-loathing disconnects and disengages us from our own body, which we feel has betrayed us because it doesn't measure up. Living in and occupying the space of our body doesn't feel safe, which means we cannot feel safe anywhere on Earth. Our body is our home. It is the temple in which our soul dwells.

How might your life change if you could look at yourself each morning and say, I love you. I love the unique beauty that I am. To cultivate beauty in the spiritual sense, a pause is required. It isn't something felt in the rush of our day and the preoccupation of our thoughts. Beauty is in the pause. Beauty is in Nature, in bringing Nature into more of your day—the flowers in your home, the garden or plants you tend to, the beauty that can bloom within you.

Create rituals of beauty. This can happen with something as simple as your morning routine: the washing of your body, the feeling of your skin, the gratitude for the flowing, cleansing water. Beauty can be a ritual. Use a sea salt scrub to purify your body as a temple would be. Use almond or coconut oil to anoint and massage your body. As you apply these, recognize it is because you love your body and want the best for your body. As you feel this beauty, you naturally want to adorn your body, a natural expression of the sacred essence you have chosen rather than a corrupted mask with which to enter into a world of deceit.

Every woman should know she is beautiful. The false prophets and preachers of beauty have corrupted us and led us astray for too long to serve their own narrow, harmful agendas. This is not the truth of beauty—and it is certainly not the truth of you.

CHAPTER TWELVE

For Sale by Owner

I FOUND A DEAD SQUIRREL in the basement of my home, the one I had bought with Phil when we first married. It was the same home I had been living in with my two daughters since we divorced. I took this as a sign to sell the house. I am no expert in spirit animals, but I did know that squirrels were the ones scurrying around for nuts, preparing for winter, saving and storing for a time when there would be none. Seeing this dead squirrel in my basement made me realize I had nothing stored away, no savings for a rainy day. With my income from working as a physical therapist and the generous child support I received from Phil each month, I could usually cover my expenses. But there were limits as to how far my money would go. Although I worked in health care, I did not have health insurance. It was not provided by my job and was an expense I could not afford. Sarabeth and Danielle were covered by their dad's plan, so I knew they were taken care of. After seeing that dead squirrel my concerns about finances became much more clear to me.

I owned a home, yet if anything were to happen to it—a water heater broke, a new appliance needed, roof repairs were necessary—the cost was beyond me. My beloved home could crush me in an instant. My younger daughter would be graduating from high school in two years. I wanted to stay in the house until she finished. I thought I would sell my home at that time and most likely leave the high cost of living in New York altogether.

At the time of my dead squirrel revelation, the housing market was saturated. So many homes were for sale in my mile-square neighborhood. Any mention of my thinking about selling was met with the same reaction. "You'll never sell your house." The market was flooded, so giving myself two years to find a buyer felt like a realistic plan. Before I put out a For Sale sign, I started cleaning. For weeks, I took to the curb garbage bags full of useless items that had been stowed in dark basement corners or stuffed on crowded garage shelves. Clothes and kitchen items, books and outgrown kids' toys were donated to Goodwill. I scrubbed behind radiators and cleaned under furniture that had been neglected for years. All the while, I imagined I was preparing the space for a new family to move in and love this old Colonial as much as I did.

After weeks of deep cleaning, I invited my two sisters over for a despacho ceremony, the highest ritual of the shamans of the Andes in Peru. Prayers for the despacho are blown into coca leaves and wrapped up like a gift, which very much reminded me of blowing wishes into dandelion seeds as a child. This same innocence and trust of a child is how a shaman prays. As in childhood, our wishes were set free to the winds. When we were children, we never worried about how our wishes would come true or what we should do to make them happen. We let the winds carry our dreams to destinations unknown. This is the same way I would come to pray with the shamans on the holy mountains of the Andes, with prayers blown into coca leaves.

My sister, Kristine, brought her daughters, Kailey and Shannon, who were the same age as my daughters, Sarabeth and Danielle. My sister, Michele, came with my niece and nephew, Mollie and Sam, who were much younger than their cousins. We sat in a circle on the grass in the small backyard of my Sea Cliff home. In the center was an open sheet of wrapping paper, and in the center of the paper, we placed red and white carnations as a bed to hold our prayers and offerings, as is the tradition in Peru. I told everyone how grateful I was that they were there, and opened up an informal space for us all to share memories of times spent in my beloved home over the years. It was my preparation for saying goodbye to the only house I had ever owned—bought with Phil and full of our hopes and dreams. It was the house both of my daughters came home to, one from Korea, the other from a nearby hospital. It was a home full of holiday meals and birthday parties, sleepovers and barbeques.

As we sat in a circle, a small pile of bay leaves, in lieu of coca leaves, sat next to me. As my sisters and daughters, nieces and nephew shared their memories, I blew the love into the bay leaves before placing them atop the carnations. There were stories of clowns making magic at birthday parties and pony rides down the driveway when Danielle turned five. There were Fourth of July barbeques with sparklers waving through the evening air. There were holiday dinners with home-made biscuits and handwritten place cards at each seat. There were chalk-drawn hopscotch games in the street and sand art on the front porch.

Once the sharing felt complete, we sprinkled grains like quinoa from the kitchen, sweets like sugar and chocolate chips, and herbs such as lavender and sage over the leaves as offerings to feed and nourish our prayers. We also added prayers for a new family to make their home here as well. The wrapping paper was then folded over all the elements holding our love, our prayers, and our hearts, and then tied up with twine like a gift. In a small fire in an outdoor pit, the despacho was burned and the prayers were released to Spirit, just like the dandelion seeds riding on the winds.

After the ceremony, I listed the house on a For Sale by Owner site. Within a few days, I received a call. In two weeks, we had a deal. I and the soon-to-be-owner of my home, who was a lawyer, negotiated the sale ourselves. I had never made a deal like this before in my life. It was a bit frightening to move so quickly since my intention had been to sell the house in two years, not two weeks. I also knew another dose of good fortune would not come along so easily, so I took a leap of faith. My daughters and I moved to an apartment we rented in an attached home nearby. The magic of that simple ceremony in the backyard of my Sea Cliff home was more powerful than anything I had ever experienced in the Andes of Peru. The freedom it gave me from the chains of owning a house would take me on another move to a place not yet known.

Clearing space helps create a more open channel for our prayers and intentions to resonate. Clutter in your outer world reflects clutter in your inner one. Think about what space in your home needs clearing up.

You don't have to tackle the garage or empty the attic. Find a drawer, a medicine chest, a shelf or even a stack of papers that need to be put in order. Clear out what you no longer need or use. Your intention should be to create space for what you want to create in your life, for whatever magic you are aligning with.

Magic is often considered an elusive art exclusive to performers, the stage, or illusionists, with us as mere mortals excluded. Magic, at its heart, is the art of creation. We are all magicians, the almighty creators behind the masterpieces of our lives. It is easy to tell ourselves we are not creative because we don't have a talent for painting or drawing or sculpture. Our life is an unlearning of this narrow definition of creativity. It is a re-remembering of our truth by discovering all the things we are not, stripped away of all the false identities we have adopted.

In the most basic sense of our lives on Earth, creative is really all that we are. We are here to create. It is our birthright and the source of our power. We are given our lives as the canvas. Our thoughts and feelings, words and deeds are the brushstrokes. Your life is the masterpiece and you are the master creating it.

CHAPTER THIRTEEN

The Goddess Aphrodite

THE FIRST TIME I KISSED Jon, he was blindfolded with a chocolate-covered cherry in his mouth. I was sitting in his lap with my legs wrapped around his hips. As the chocolate candy broke open, the sticky sweetness that oozed from it sealed our first kiss. I had been aching to kiss him for months.

I met Jon in 2006 shortly after attending a weekend of feminine empowerment at Kripalu in the Berkshires. Alberto Villoldo and Marcela Lobos of the Four Winds Society led the gathering, with about a hundred fifty men and women attending. To my surprise, a woman I knew from the trance dance and breathwork world in New York City was also there. After my divorce, I spent nearly every other Saturday night, when my daughters were with their dad, at Osho active meditations, trance dances or group breathwork sessions in New York City. Trinity led dance circles for emotional release in the same spaces, attended by many of the same people, which is how I knew her.

Creating what Alberto and Marcela called sacred drama to honor the goddess was part of the weekend. I had never participated in a sacred drama before and wasn't even sure what it was. In fact, I was woefully unfamiliar with goddesses in general. I had no thought of participating until Trinity approached me and suggested we create something together. I would never have the guts to do something like that on my own. I felt emboldened by having a partner, so I said, "Yes."

We signed up for one of the limited number of slots, but for some reason I don't remember, Trinity abruptly left the retreat and I had to create and perform the sacred drama on my own. I was terrified by the fact that I knew nothing about this, had no experience with it, and also had no idea what other people would be doing. Although I could have dropped out entirely, it seemed worse to have spent my time and money driving hundreds of miles to empower my divine and sacred feminine only to return home disempowered. I decided to go ahead with it despite my deep insecurities and incessant fear.

Aphrodite was the only name my mind could extract from its limited data bank on goddesses. All I knew was that she was a goddess of sexuality and eroticism, which felt about as far as you could get from who I was then. My sexuality was never something I'd felt comfortable with. Before Phil, I never had sustained relationships with men. As a young woman, my search for love was tied to the belief that I had to give my body away to get someone to love me. Love and sex were entangled in a confused kinship that severed my heart from my sexuality. Aphrodite seemed like the perfect goddess to invoke since my sexuality felt crippled. Our sacred drama had no rules or guidelines other than a ten-minute time slot in which to honor and represent the goddess we chose.

I decided for my sacred drama to write a poem, an invocation to Aphrodite, and to dance. After my divorce, dance had become one of my most liberating and sensual practices. I had never studied dance as a child. Never once had I been in a recital. Trance dancing though was different. It was free-form movement that let energy move through your body in response to the music. There was no choreography or rehearsal so essentially there was nothing for me to practice. I went to Kripalu's gift shop and bought an instrumental dance CD with a Moroccan beat reminiscent of the percussive rhythms used in trance dancing. I would start the sacred drama by reading the poem I had written and then dance to a track on the CD, trusting it would all come together through the divine guidance of Aphrodite.

The final day of our retreat was reserved for the sacred drama. As I waited my turn, I could see that what others were doing was highly prepared—well-rehearsed skits they'd written, original songs sung with acoustic guitar.

Then came my turn in the center of the circle.

The choices in my suitcase were limited, but I'd selected my clothes carefully: a wrap silk skirt of sage green florals tied around my waist, black capri leggings, and a black fitted camisole. My thick brown curls hung loose to my shoulders. I was terrified. A hundred fifty strangers surrounded me. I had written a poem to read but then what? I had no idea what I was going to do.

My CD was cued up. I sat cross-legged with poem in hand and read my invocation to Aphrodite:

The way to get love was give my body away,
Using sex like a beggar,
Hungry in need.
Sexuality in exile,
Banished from me.
Driven away on the wounds of shame,
Ugliness living deep inside me.
I invoke Aphrodite.
Goddess of Beauty.
Goddess of Love.
To dance within me my femininity.
To enjoy my body
And its sensual pleasures.
Let my beauty rise up
In light to be seen.
An intimate expression
Of my vulnerability.
Aphrodite,
The most sacred
Aspect of me.

The music started. I left the poem on the floor and stood up. Slowly I started to twirl. It came so spontaneously that it surprised even me. I had no idea where it came from. The spinning quickened with the beat. My arms extended out in a heart-opening gesture to those around me. My skirt and hair began to fly in the wind. I felt like a whirling dervish. My mind settled as the movement created a core of stillness with everything spinning around it. In this stillness, a thought dropped into my mind like a pebble in water rippling into perfect concentric circles.

> *"I cannot believe you are standing in the middle of a hundred and fifty people, and all you are doing is spinning."*

As if spinning was not enough. As if I should be entertaining people with high kicks and complicated dance moves. Then the clapping started, the circle clapping in time to the music, an affirmation to the dance. I became the whirl, the energy that has spun through eons of time, ancient and primordial. I was both movement and stillness, music and silence. The music stopped. The sacred drama ended. People were applauding.

I stepped outside the circle with gratitude. Grateful I had showed up. Grateful that something had emerged as I stood in that space. Those few moments there were a mystery to me. I had been held in a state of grace, a grace born from trusting that what I needed in the moment would be there. What arose in the moment was organic, spontaneous, and the strangers around that circle responded. There was no script, no plan. It was as if each of us had tasted a sip of the divine, and for a moment, Aphrodite danced in each of us. One month later, I met Jon. I had no idea when I stepped into that circle that it would become a portal to an erotic awakening, by teaching me where trust could take me.

In the same way that feminine empowerment had led me to Kripalu, it also was what motivated my journeys to Peru. The

Divine Feminine can be mind-boggling, almost greater than I can comprehend, and even more challenging to inhabit in ourselves when the sacred beings inside us are so obscured by the crush of our everyday world. The goddess represents the Divine Feminine in all of her aspects. Working with goddess archetypes like Aphrodite and Lakshmi can open the door to accessing the Divine Feminine. Connecting with the ancient wisdom of a goddess archetype can deepen the awareness of your divinity and help cultivate qualities to bring forth in yourself and begin to guide your life along higher dimensions. What a blessing it could be to learn to trust the cycles of life in their own natural flow instead of always trying to control them.

If you feel called in any way to work with the energy of the goddess, you may want to consider buying a deck of goddess cards, with images and messages of what the goddesses represent. I have always loved oracle or tarot cards as a way to receive messages. Before I sent this manuscript to my editor, I pulled Lakshmi, a Hindu goddess of wealth and good fortune, from a deck of goddess cards. The message on the card read: "Bright Future: Stop worrying. Everything is going to be fine." Sometimes the cards can encourage us, sometimes they give us thoughts to contemplate. Spirit had certainly sent me that message before, back when I was lost on the mountain with my dog, Jethro.

Having an altar can be a beautiful way to create an alignment with a goddess archetype. The space you dedicate for your altar doesn't have to be large. You can designate it with a cloth. Your goddess card can be placed on your altar. If you don't have a card, any items that might represent this goddess for you can be added. For Lakshmi, the goddess of wealth and good fortune, for instance, coins or money may be placed on an altar.

A candle is always helpful on an altar. The act of lighting it brings light to our intentions. It reminds us of the sacred and brings the element of fire to cleanse and purify. You can include fresh flowers or items that have special meaning to you. You can write a prayer or invocation to your goddess. Spend some time with your altar each day, whether it is lighting a candle, adding a fresh flower, or saying a prayer as you let the mystery of the goddess inform your life.

CHAPTER FOURTEEN

When Soul Rises to Lips

THE MOST MYSTICAL RELATIONSHIP OF my life started in one of the most mundane ways. My friend Lorraine thought Jon and I would be a good match. Lorraine was the founder and owner of the Yoga Flow studio in Glen Head, Long Island. Besides being an exceptional yoga teacher, she was also a physical therapist. Although my approach to physical therapy was more traditional, our shared interests in healing and yoga created a kinship between us.

Jon was a student of Lorraine's at Yoga Flow. "All the women love Jon," she told me. "I think the two of you would hit it off." Lorraine arranged for us to meet over dinner one night with another couple from her studio joining us. I had never been on a blind date before, but I trusted my friend. We met at a Thai restaurant in Port Washington, a wealthy hamlet on the North Shore of Long Island overlooking Manhasset Bay. Jon was a very good-looking guy, someone who caught your attention when he entered the room. He stood six feet tall with thick, graying hair that he pushed back off his face. It was just long enough to wrap behind his ears and fall slightly above his shoulders. Small silver hoops pierced each ear lobe. He had deep blue eyes and looked as if he hadn't shaved in a day or two. He was sexy and rugged and, surprisingly, single.

As we settled into our seats around the table, the conversation focused on Jon's recent return from a week-long Zen Buddhist meditation retreat in California with his former wife. The other couple at the table were quite interested in Jon and the retreat. He had moved back to New York after two decades in California, now living with his aging mother in her home on the North Shore. He had a daughter in San Francisco. He was a photographer but no longer working professionally. I wasn't involved in much of the conversation that night. By the time dinner ended, neither Jon nor I seemed to have any interest in the other.

After the weekend at Kripalu, I felt driven to bring my dance of Aphrodite to some form of a more tangible creative expression, as if I could somehow capture the divine magic of the moment. My idea was to make a short video intertwining the words of the poem with naked images of myself which I would make available to friends and close acquaintances. Being photographed naked felt both extremely vulnerable and intensely liberating. I wanted to feel naked, physically and emotionally, after what felt like a lifetime of living in a suit of armor.

I reached out to talk about my idea with Jon since he was a photographer. I had no romantic interest in him, so calling to talk about naked photos felt very professional. We met at a local juice bar, and I shared with Jon my experience at Kripalu and the idea of intertwining photos with the poem. He had no interest, feeling that setting up photo shoots was a hassle he had left behind. He suggested that my teenage daughters take the pictures. When I told him it seemed absurd that they would want to see their mother naked, it made my original intention more clear, and he changed his mind. We set a date. Perhaps there should have been some alarm at his change of heart. Even though I had just met him over our failed dinner date, I was trusting my desire to bring this project to life. Meeting a photographer felt serendipitous.

I gathered silk scarves from my closets and bought roses from the florist, things I thought would enhance the sensuality of the photos. I prepared my dining room for the photo shoot, a room where the family had gathered for birthday parties and holiday dinners. I cleared out the pine wood dining table and ladder back chairs. I rolled up the area rug that covered the center of the room leaving the wood floor bare. When the doorbell rang I was wearing a robe with nothing underneath. Jon arrived laden with cameras, lights, and tripods. It all felt very professional. Since I had no interest in him it felt easy to disrobe for the photos. The encounter was so far beyond my normal parameters as a divorced woman with two teenage daughters that it felt exhilarating and empowering to be taking charge of my life in such a provocative way.

Jon told me how to stand and where to look while I assumed various positions lying on my back or with a silk scarf draped over my body. At one point, while I was lying on my stomach with the tops of my feet crossed over each other, Jon began putting rose petals along my spine. There was something so delicate in how he placed them on my body. When he reached the base of my spine, an erotic charge surged through my groin. I had never felt anything like that before. The touch was barely a whisper, but an electric current coursed up my spine in excitement. I felt sexy and seductive and embarrassed all at once. Years later, Jon would tell me that he too felt the same erotic charge.

By the time the photo shoot ended, my feelings about Jon had been utterly altered. I wanted to see more of him. We spent the next few weeks sitting in front of a computer screen in his mother's basement cropping and editing the images he had taken. Sitting next to him looking at naked photos of myself felt like the most natural thing in the world. My desire for Jon was rising, but he still seemed to have no interest. When the project was over, the thought of not seeing him again was crushing.

Relationships since my divorce had been pretty much sexual in nature. There were no commitments and no one I'd become attached to. I was feeling liberated from the obligatory sex through most of my marriage. I was tired, though, of sleeping with men with no emotional investment. I suggested to Jon that we practice Contact Yoga together. In Contact Yoga you and your partner essentially become one posture.

The support or weight of one body against the other allows a posture to go deeper than if practicing on your own. As two bodies become one, the breath begins to sync. The practice becomes one of intimacy, an art I was completely flawed in. We started a weekly Contact Yoga practice in the same room in my home where the naked photo shoot took place, this time with yoga mats on the floor. It was a new way for me to explore being physical with someone. No one was naked. Our clothes provided a boundary between us, yet the movements and postures were very intimate. After four weeks of practice, I definitely wanted to be closer to him.

At the end of one of our Contact Yoga sessions, I was sitting in his lap with my legs wrapped around his hips. Our heads were bowed slightly and our foreheads were in contact. Our lips were a breath away. I could feel a kiss rising, the desire burning in my body. As I leaned in ever so slightly, Jon felt like stone. He did not want to kiss. I remember him saying, "I don't want to be in another situation where I don't know what I'm doing."

Another situation? Jon's old lovers, I would learn, never seemed to go away.

His reluctance to kiss did not end our practice. We continued to fold and bend and wrap our bodies around each other each week. The fit of our bodies and the deep physical connection created through Contact Yoga fed my desire to kiss him. It was hard to believe that Jon was not feeling the same way. He was agreeable and open to our ongoing practice but seemed to default to a position of passivity when it came to initiating anything further. I had never been with a man who did not make the first move. The only way there would be anything between us was if I made it happen. This was all new territory for me.

I came up with an idea, and asked Jon for help. I decided to offer a Valentine's Day workshop at our friend Lorraine's yoga studio. Even though Jon and I were not a couple, he agreed to help me with a Valentine's workshop. The flyer read:

"Love should be your interior core of breathing.
It should be as natural as breathing.
In fact love has the same relationship to the soul
as breathing has to the body."
OSHO

Come spend a sacred evening in celebration of your Beloved!
Connect more deeply to your partner
through the heart opening touch of Thai Massage.
Experience the pleasure in both giving and receiving
while you heighten your sensitivity
to the energetic presence of your partner.
Explore the more subtle dimensions of each other
through guided exchanges of breath and touch
and enjoy a deeper connection in body, mind and soul.

Thai massage was the foundation of my work in physical therapy. My first encounter with it came through images in a book which would ultimately lead to traveling to Thailand with my two young daughters. The techniques resonated immediately. Thai massage stretches the body through passive yoga positions in an energetic dance between giver and receiver. I loved teaching Thai massage. The movements felt good for both the person giving as well as the one receiving it. It was perfect for a couples workshop. Jon was a highly sensual man. He enjoyed receiving Thai massage as we prepared for the workshop however, I didn't let him know everything I had planned for the evening.

The event took place the Friday evening after Valentine's Day. The studio felt sacred and romantic, with candles providing the only light as sensual instrumentals played softly on a CD in the background. Jon and I sat cross-legged on the floor at the head of the room with the other couples joining us to form a circle. We introduced ourselves and began the evening by having the members of the couples face each other. They extended their left hand to place it over their partner's heart. The partner placed their right hand on top. They sat with hands over hearts while gazing gently into each other's eyes. They were asked to share what they appreciate about their partner, men going first.

After these exchanges, the couples then turned to sit back to back with as much of their head, hips, and spines touching as possible. With eyes closed, they began to bring their breaths into unison. On an exhale, the men bowed forward while the woman relaxed back onto their partner's spine. After a few moments of breathing together, the positions were reversed. You could feel a blanket of warmth envelop the room as these opening rituals took each person deeper into their own bodies, helping to shed the activity of the day while heightening the awareness of each other.

We then moved into the exchange of Thai massage. The women lay on their backs atop yoga mats and blankets. Jon, as he was my model for the demonstration, laid down on his mat. The men were led through a short and sensual Thai massage routine. Positions were switched as the men then became the receivers. Once the couples had completed their exchanges, they returned to sitting, facing each other now with the woman on the man's lap. I passed out bandanas to the women to blindfold their partners. I did the same to Jon. I gave each woman a chocolate-covered cherry as they sat in their partner's lap. The men were asked to open their mouths.

On a silent cue, the women placed the cherry in their own mouth and then, holding it between their teeth, let their partner also take it in their mouth. I did the same with Jon. As I bit down on the candy, the chocolate shell broke apart. The cherry syrup oozed into our mouths. I had constructed the entire event for this moment. I had been aching to kiss him ever since he laid those rose petals on my back. The only salvation for my shameless manipulation was the eagerness with which Jon returned the deep longing I felt. As the sticky syrup swirled in our mouths, our tongues wrapped around each other in a ravenous union. This time Jon kissed me back. It felt like a kiss I had been waiting my whole life to receive.

As sexual beings, our erotic energy is the most potent force we feel in our body. The spiritual revolution of our times is the awakening of the Divine Feminine in women. This was made so clear in the teachings on light from Doña Aleja, a master shaman or altomesayok, when I was in Peru. A silver cord of light, she told us, runs through the central channel of a woman. For men, the channel is gold. As man and woman merge in lovemaking, their bodies become filled with light. At orgasm, the silver light of women and the golden light of men alchemize to create violet, the light of creation.

At this moment, lovers are exalted as god and goddess in a sacred and powerful dance of creation. We are born of our biological mother and father, but we are also born of the divine god and goddess. Know this to be so. Elevate your understanding of sexuality to this exalted level of light. See yourself as the goddess and imagine setting your dreams free on the waves of your orgasm.

LGBTQ men and women are special, Doña Aleja said, because they have both silver and gold cords. With many spiritual traditions, those in same-sex relationships are highly respected and revered as "Two Spirits." Together, she taught, the gold and silver cords become the violet light of creation, illuminating the special role of women. "It is important that women know these teachings of light," Doña Aleja said. "Women create life past the age of conception. We must teach women to have this knowledge of light in the moment of creation. Women are the givers of life so they can help to change the world."

Doña Aleja was also clear about the myth of libido's drying up after menopause, as if the power of the creative force evaporates. "Although our sexual energy is no longer seeking procreation," she said, "this does not mean that the power of that energy has dried up or disappeared. A menopausal woman enters the most potent expression of her libido. Once her energy is no longer outward in its search to conceive, it turns upward to the heavens as a celestial uterus."

This "celestial uterus" represents the fullness of the feminine power of creation, a power so great that for those who cannot control it, they must distort it. The false creation stories twist our psyches into diminishing our power to create. From the beginning with Adam and Eve, women have been blamed and shamed as sluts and whores when they acknowledge the erotic power of their bodies. What we express of ourselves sexually is what is at the root of creation. No matter your age, know that your sexuality can be your most potent creative energy. If you are holding onto any shame about your erotic body, let it burn in a simple fire ceremony. Light a candle. Blow your intentions to release the shame into a toothpick and let it burn.

CHAPTER FIFTEEN

Dark Night of the Soul

I CANNOT FIND A WORD to name my relationship with Jon. We have been the best of friends and the sexiest of lovers. We have also been estranged from these connections. Boyfriend and girlfriend always sounded ill-fitting. We never married.

After my marriage with Phil ended the only thing left to untangle at the end was the legal connection. How do you divide up the assets? What agreements do you determine regarding your children? Who stays in the house and who goes? It was heartless and painful. Married was not something I wanted to be again.

Without any kind of commitment or even language defining our relationship I was often unsure of who we were to each other. One thing though did feel true. From its roots in manipulation to its wellsprings of magic, my relationship with Jon was destined. When I met him, I was a forty-five-year-old divorced mother of two teenage daughters working as a physical therapist. Jon was ten years older than me living with his aging mother.

My relationship with him became the most consistent one since my divorce, yet it was always kept at a distance from the rest of my life. Jon did not spend time with my daughters. He did not attend family gatherings or holiday dinners.

Perhaps the best way to understand our relationship was through the poetry. Never had I known the sensual depths of a man to run as deep as they did with Jon. In our early years together, we spent a lot of our time in his makeshift bedroom in his mother's attic. On one side was what we called Jon's zendo. It was there we would practice yoga on rolled out mats or meditate together on zafu cushions. Walled off on the other side of the attic was the bedroom. Against one wall was a small twin bed. Opposite it was a tiny dresser with a mirror hanging over it. Out the window, cardinals perched on the upper branches of an old oak tree. We made love in the tiny twin bed.

In the days we were not together, we sent erotic love letters to fill the space of longing that we felt while apart. I had never written love letters before, especially ones so erotically charged, but Jon had awakened a sexual passion in me I never knew was there. The longing could only be filled by the intoxicating love letters full of our passionate desires and erotic fantasies that would fill the gap until our bodies devoured each other once again.

We were discovering sexual pleasures and bodily freedoms in ways that were new to us both. Our first years together seemed transcendent. We were amorous explorers of each other's hearts, minds, and bodies, and yet the intensity in our coming together also seemed to be what drove us apart. Our passion was like an inferno that would swallow us whole. Although it was unspoken, we both seemed afraid we would each lose our individual self if we committed to being a couple. We danced between an erotic love affair and devastating breakups when we became too afraid of being too close—and thus being too vulnerable.

That was the pattern, engulfed in flames or fearing our own intimacy. The ache we felt when apart would draw us back together again as if the other person could fill the dark hole of the demons that stalked us. What the demons would never let us do is fully open up our hearts—which would require overcoming the traumas and fear that seemed to be dragged from every relationship that had come before.

After one of many breakups, Jon sent an email: "I think I teeter-totter in a way that must be hard to see which way I am leaning from day to day. In a way that you really don't know if you have my support, my embrace. If I am just biding my time here." Those words would hold an even deeper relevance decades later when his decisions would make his meaning clear.

About two years after our chocolate-covered cherry kiss, Jon left for Hawaii to immerse himself in a kundalini yoga teacher training on the Big Island. We called it his magical mystery tour. Our future felt more uncertain than ever. I was filled with doubt that the relationship was solid enough to endure the distance between us. I thought for sure I would never see him again. What happened while he was away surprised us both. The erotic fire burned even hotter. We wrote poems full of the desire to feel our bodies arching together in pleasure, to feel our souls rising to lips. We sent naked videos arousing each other's pleasure. Jon was the sexiest man I had ever known, with the romantic soul of a poet. The distance brought us even closer.

He returned from Hawaii as a teacher, and much of our time was now spent practicing kundalini. Jon started teaching Sunday morning classes at Lorraine's studio, and during the week, I helped him practice the *kriyas* he was planning to teach. These are a sort of prescriptive set of yoga exercises developed by Yogi Bhajan that are done for specific times with specific intentions. I had taken kundalini classes over the years, but my daily yoga practice was an intuitive one, not adhering to any specific tradition.

Kundalini now became the yogic thread between us. We sat in Jon's zendo on sheepskin mats chanting the *Ong Namo Guru Dev Namo* mantra and practicing Breath of Fire. I took Jon's kundalini yoga class every Sunday. The studio at Yoga Flow was filled with natural light through the nearly floor-to-ceiling windows covering the west wall. After class, Jon always had yogi tea with ginger cookies waiting outside the studio, so students lingered in the lobby before leaving. We created workshops together for students at Yoga Flow interweaving Kundalini yoga, shamanic ceremony, and Thai massage with the intention of nurturing loving, passionate relationships. Still, amid this close connection of our provocative reunions, the devastating separations would continue. The pattern remained, until years later, our worst break up finally brought me to a descent into the dark night of the soul.

By this time, Jon's mother, Susan, was on hospice. She had gone from living a vibrant life for eighty-plus years to lying in a hospital bed in a second-floor bedroom at home. Having Jon there was a blessing which allowed her the dignity to remain in her home as the end of life drew near.

Jon was a natural caregiver. He took loving care of his mom, administering medications, giving her foot massages, helping her dress and bathe as needed. Any time we had together was spent with her. Our relationship shaped itself around the priority of her needs whether it was making trips to see doctors, offering bedside massages, or finding ways to ease her suffering. When Jon first moved in with his mother, she was independent, with a life of her own and a circle of friends that had been with her since childhood. She had lymphoma, and always thought she was going to die soon. Every time I was at the house, she wanted me to check her pulse. I think she saw me as part of the medical profession, giving me some credentials to assure her she was going to be fine. Now, I was sitting beside her as she lay in her bed. She still wanted me to check her pulse. I assured her it was good. I rubbed her feet and held her hand. She loved opera, and Jon was sure to have it playing often.

Then one evening, standing in the hallway outside his mother's bedroom, Jon told me, "I can't do this anymore." He meant our relationship. There were lapses between us when we separated before, but this felt like I was being severed from his life just when his mother's own life was at a precipice. The shock made me numb. There was no conversation. He had made up his mind. I went back to his mother's bedroom. My heart was breaking. I kept a smile on my face as I said goodbye to her for what I knew was the last time. I couldn't tell her I would not be back, or that her son had just broken up with me. I couldn't sort through the shock and sorrow, so I held her hand, kissed her forehead, and said good night.

A few days later, Susan died. Jon told me by email. I was devastated. The deluge of grief was unbearable—for both her death and the death of our relationship. As his family, friends, and lovers from the past gathered for her service, I was left alone with my grief. I had sat with his mother as the life force slowly drained from her body and yet was forsaken when the ending came.

The death of Jon's mother seemed to crack my heart open to an insufferable grief compounded by the death of my father a few months earlier. When I received the news, I remembered thinking, "My father just died and I don't feel a thing." I saw my dad about once a year after he and my mother moved to Florida twenty-five years earlier. Even when my parents would come to visit family in New York, I don't recall having a one-on-one conversation with him. We never talked on the phone. I loved my dad, but we did not have much of a relationship. Still, the death of a parent seemed like I should *feel something*. I did not feel his loss from my life because he did not feel as if he were a part of my life.

The death of Jon's mother and the death of our relationship left me inconsolable. The grief of losing Jon seemed to increase the sense of loss from my father's death, not so much because we'd been close or I missed my relationship with him but just because he was my dad. His role in my life could never be filled by anyone else.

An isolating loneliness engulfed me even though to the outside world, nothing seemed different. I tended to my daughters, took care of the home, and continued to see patients. Although I carried on as if nothing had happened, my inner world became an unrecognizable shell. Every demon that had ever made me feel like an outsider, unwanted and unloved, was unleashed from its dark hiding place for me to now face alone. It seemed like the dark tunnel of madness had swallowed me whole, and I had no idea how to find a way out.

A few miles from where I lived I did have a sanctuary, a three-square-mile nature preserve amid the suburban homes and gridlock. It was there that I went to pray, not in the traditional ways of a church or Western culture but in the rituals of the shamans with whom I had climbed the holy mountains of Peru. I walked barefoot along the well-trodden dirt trails winding through dense forests of red oaks, tulip trees, and poplars. With three bay leaves in hand simulating the coca leaf *k'intus* of Peru, I blew every sorrow in my heart, every ache in my bones, and every darkness in my soul into the leaves. I waded through the chilly, salty waters of Long Island Sound in November until my legs were numb from the cold. I followed the dirt trail on the shore until I could feel the ground beneath my bare feet again. The Earth was holding me, her elements cleansing me. It was as if everything I had ever learned from the shamans of Peru was being put to the test, to drive the teachings deeper into my bones.

Those teachings were becoming an embodied way of walking in the world rather than an intellectual concept. By the time I was ready to leave the woods that day, my anguish had eased. I had risen from an internal collapse whose weight felt crushing. The mystery of this communion is beyond me. To the mind, it makes no sense to breathe into leaves, wade in cold water until your feet are numb, or walk barefoot on the earth for comfort, yet our Mother Earth was healing me, holding me, and sustaining me through a crisis of soul. I felt as if I was weaving my body and soul back to her in this walk upon the Earth as her daughter.

I sent Jon an email when I returned home, expressing my condolence. I shared with him my own sorrow at being alone after tending to his mother's needs as she neared the end of her life. The loss I felt at no longer being a part of his life was hard to bear. There was no invitation to his mother's funeral, nor was I expecting one, but in their family's Jewish tradition, the family sits *shiva* for seven days. After the psychic clearing I experienced from my time in the woods, it felt important for me to show up. I knew Jon would never tell his family or any of his mother's friends that we'd broken up. Any questions as to why I was not gathering at the home with other family and friends would be left unspoken. Knowing Jon's mother over the years also had meant knowing her circle of lifelong friends. His mother felt important enough for me to make an effort to be joining them there at the house.

Praying in the woods as the shamans would do in Peru had brought me an internal shift. The experience left me steadfast and resolute in my decision to be at the gathering. I returned home from the woods, baked a lasagna, and drove to his mother's the next day.

The home was filled with family, friends, and neighbors mingling through the first-floor rooms when I arrived. As I made my way from the front door to the kitchen, I saw Jon talking with his aunt next to the bannister. Our eyes locked for a moment. I knew he was uncomfortably shocked to see me. I continued on into the kitchen and offered the lasagna to his brother, who was grateful for the gesture. I spent a short time with the people I felt closest to, mainly his mother's friends. I left without a word to Jon. Soon after his mother's funeral, I received an email from him that surprised me: "I had to drop my head in shame for excluding you from these rituals of grieving." A hawk, he said, had flown overhead during the drive to the cemetery. "I imagine it was you," he wrote. "A display of the freedom and the power you are finding. The majestic beauty that I fear I may never meet again." There was nothing for him to fear. Despite all our breakups, all I wanted was him.

A crisis of the soul cannot be healed with logic and sense. Although I knew I was in my body and on this Earth, I felt completely disconnected from both. We can go to a gym and lift weights to make our muscles stronger, but how do we strengthen our muscles of faith, our relationship to Spirit? Through the darkest of nights, when it feels as if no one is listening or cares, when our hopelessness and despair feel inconsolable, it is faith that provides the bridge and faith is strengthened through prayer.

A conduit of breath carries the shaman's prayer to nature, returned to the elements and offered to Spirit. In the mountains of Peru, three coca leaves are traditionally used to create a prayer holder or k'intu. Any element of nature—stones, crystals, plants, petals—can carry your prayers in this way. We hold a prayer in our heart and feel gratitude for its presence. We use our breath to blow this intent into a prayer holder. The breath is the energetic pathway on which the prayer travels. Whatever we are looking to release, let go of, or set in motion can be offered by exhaling into a k'intu. Your prayer holder is then offered back to the Earth and can be buried, burned in a fire, released to the waters, or carried by the winds. We weave ourselves back to the land and deepen our connection with nature in this way.

Whatever you are holding in your heart may be offered as prayer. This can be weights and sorrows, burdens and fears that you feel you have no one to share with. There may be no one in your life whom you believe you can trust, and that you must carry everything alone. All of this can be offered in prayer, emptied from you heart and mind to your prayer holder. The heaviness in your heart does not have to be named, the tension in your jaw doesn't need a meaning. Beyond thoughts, the density that you feel in your body is something you can empty through your breath and release to your prayer holder.

This is what I was doing in my time in the woods after Jon's mother died. What I felt wasn't something I could articulate or that made sense to the rational mind. I was not in its realm. It was the realm of prayer, not analysis, that pulled me through a dark night when there seemed to be no other way out.

CHAPTER SIXTEEN

A Blessing in White

WERE IT NOT FOR A blizzard in New York, I never would have moved to New Mexico. After the death of Jon's mother, our relationship severed, yet slivers of connection remained. I was in the midst of self-publishing my first book, *A Structure for Spirit*. Jon had been helping me through the project by generously providing beautiful photographs for the cover and inside pages, which we discussed in intermittent email exchanges.

It was late November when his mother died. I didn't see him again until January when I delivered my dog TJ, a tan and white Cavalier King Charles Spaniel, whom he'd agreed to watch while I went to a gathering in Louisiana of the women I traveled to Peru with. Jon was the ultimate dog lover and dogs thoroughly and wholeheartedly loved him back.

On the night before my trip, snow began lightly falling. As I drove the twenty minutes to his mother's home, snow was piling up along the roads. The snow was quickly becoming a blizzard, one that would bring the city to a full-blown halt. By the time I got to the house, the windswept drifts were taller than TJ, who stood no more than a foot high. Carrying him up the walkway, I could feel my heart pounding. As I waited for Jon to answer my knock, I thought my beating heart would burst through the wall of my chest.

We embraced awkwardly, for the first time in two months. I was extremely grateful he was taking care of TJ, which seemed to override everything else I was feeling. Then, a message on the phone alerted me that my flight had been canceled. We turned on the TV and saw that LaGuardia Airport had been shut down. Jon and I were unexpectedly stuck together at his mother's home. The weekend I was starting had been cleared of plans, everything I needed was in my luggage in the car. It was as if the world had hermetically sealed us together in the chasm of a snowstorm that felt miraculous.

As we hunkered down to ride out the blizzard, we built a fire in the fireplace and started making something to eat. Cooking together, with the fire burning in the living room, weakened the walls that our hearts had built to keep from feeling the grief and separation. Our hands brushed each other ever so lightly reaching toward the sink. The desire for Jon burned in my belly just as it had when he first laid the rose petals on my back. The fire between us reignited. Our bodies were ravenously wrapped around each other once again.

We called it our snow blessing. Had it not been for that blizzard, I know I never would have seen Jon again. He was preparing to sell his mother's home and move to New Mexico, though I didn't really understand why. Although manipulation had been the first step that led us dancing in erotic waters, the only thing that carried us through the years afterward was magic. The snow blessing was the first of many divine interventions that seemed destined to keep Jon and me in each other's lives.

The next few months were spent preparing for Jon's move. The house was sold, and little by little, his belongings were packed and stowed until they would eventually be crammed into a moving truck. As he headed west to his new home, I was on a plane to Peru.

I went to visit him in New Mexico about a month later, the first chance I had. We hiked and made love and cooked dinners in his home. We had no idea how this long-distance situation was going to work out, and just didn't talk about it. We didn't know what we wanted or what was possible. I couldn't figure out how to be with him. New Mexico seemed so far from my daughters, my family, and everything I had ever known. Yet I had heard myself ruminating to people over the past few years, "I've lived in New York my whole life. I wonder what it would be like to live somewhere else?" I didn't know where that somewhere else might be, but a part of me was already leaving New York behind.

In August, I visited Jon again for my birthday. We had an elegant dinner followed by a night at the dramatic open-air Santa Fe Opera enveloped by the mountains and sunset-filled skies. The whole evening was proof of the many ways Jon had of creating magic. I couldn't tell you what opera we saw, but I left feeling like a goddess that night.

My final visit with Jon came in October, the most enchanting time of year in New Mexico. The arid heat of summer has passed. The skies are cloudless blue. The cottonwoods lining the Chama River begin turning with golden majesty. As soon as I arrived, I began feeling a distance between us. We didn't make love right away, which seemed odd for a couple who hadn't seen each other for two months. Instead, we drove the rough and dusty thirteen-mile dirt road to the beautiful monastery of Christ in the Desert. We visited the small chapel served by the Benedictines who had lived there since 1964. We walked the paths to the Chama River past fields of hops that would eventually be sold as Monks' Ale. We visited the scattered homes of potters and weavers, painters and sculptors in the annual Abiquiu Studio Tour. There were no plans made for another visit. My heart felt empty when I left but I said nothing. What upset us was left unsaid; that was our way.

Once I returned home, my relationship with Jon seemed to come into focus. I was by myself on a remote stretch of highway in upstate New York when the reality hit. I was four hours into a six-hour drive to Oswego, New York, to visit my oldest daughter, Sarabeth, for a Family and Friends weekend at college when the engine of my old Ford Taurus had died. As I sat waiting for the tow truck, I knew I could not call Jon. Although there'd been no "official" breakup, he felt gone from my life. He was thousands miles of away and obviously couldn't help with the car. But it was the fact that I couldn't count on him in a time of need for emotional support, or even to share what had happened. It was more than just miles that separated us.

I called Jon once I returned home after the weekend in Oswego with a rental car.

"Are we breaking up?"

"Yes," he answered.

There was nothing more to say.

A few weeks later, I received an email expressing his loneliness, his heartache, his grief at having let go of the beauty we had. At first, I didn't reply, as if waiting could delay what was dying between us; when I did, I told him he had been "the dearest delight in my life." The loss felt devastating. I missed everything about him from the sound of his voice to the touch of his hands. I missed the magic and beauty of New Mexico, which felt as if it had been woven into my soul. My heart had been broken more times than I could count, as the pattern of our relationship kept playing out time and again.

I believed I would never see Jon again, yet I felt tethered to him in ways I couldn't see coming by an invisible cord that I simply couldn't cut. Just as I had written endless love letters to him, I now wrote good-bye letters which I would never send. So much of our relationship felt unresolved, but in the healing I had to go through, writing helped. If your life has relationships where pain, anger, bitterness, or resentment keeps lingering, writing can be a powerful tool.

Write non-stop—so that your words keep flowing continuously, so they bypass your mind which is always waiting to judge and edit; write with the truth that is in your heart. Keeping the pen moving (or the fingers hitting the keyboard) is what is most important. You may reach a point when it feels you can't write anymore. Just keep going. You may think that what you are writing doesn't make sense. Just keep writing. You might feel the words you're putting down have nothing to do with the person you are writing about. Just keep on.

You are not looking to create a literary masterpiece. Don't think about grammar or punctuation or spelling. If you feel stuck, write whatever you notice in that moment. You might write that you feel stuck, or that you don't want to write anymore. Your words may repeat themselves. Just keep writing. Often, places of resistance like these hold the deepest truths—if we just keep writing. *Often, the real reason you want to stop is that you're getting so much closer to a pain you want to avoid.* Just keep writing.

As our emotions move us through these places, there may be rage or sorrow or tears. This is good. You are releasing the energy you have used to hold back your feelings. When your letter is finished, you can fold it up and blow in a prayer of thanks.

Gratitude may feel difficult, but at a time like this, we should realize all the things that happened that have shaped us, have made us each the person we were meant to be, the individuals we are becoming. And we should feel thankful for these things. As much as you may wish some were different, recognize them as all part of your soul's journey. It is easy to be grateful when things feel like they're going our way, but offering gratitude for the challenges, pain, and obstacles in our lives can be one of the most difficult things we do.

This is a lesson that the passing of time has taught me. It requires our hearts to stretch wide. Holding our pain, as well as our joy, in gratitude gives us the vantage point from the mountaintop. It opens our spiritual eye so we are not continuously looking at life through the eyes of our wounds.

Our pain can become a source of our power. Bringing forth what we have been hiding or holding back is how we transcend these painful challenges. As we delve into the depths of our darkness, we can discover a new light within ourselves. This meeting of darkness and light is the source of creation.

A writing practice can help bring it forth. You can do this with letters—there's no need to ever send them—but in whatever form, do it non-stop, organically. Intent is not needed. Just write. The purpose isn't to be linear; it's to get to a place that you may not have known. This can be a ritual you continue to practice, with each letter revealing a deeper experience as layers of armor are shed. You can continue to transcend the roots of pain, and rise to higher vantage points on your spiritual journey so you can see from a wider perspective.

CHAPTER SEVENTEEN

Ascension to Joy

IN 2011, I JOINED FACEBOOK. This may not seem like a pivotal moment in life, but it led to many connections that steered my future in ways I could never see coming. It was a time when innocence could still be found by scrolling through posts. I had been resistant to joining, unsure what the purpose of social media was, but everyone seemed to be using it. I had recently published *A Structure for Spirit,* the book Don Andreas saw in my coca leaf reading that I had written. Promoting myself didn't feel comfortable, but Facebook seemed like the most expedient way to reach potential readers. I created a Facebook page named after the book, which led to reconnecting with old high school friends, becoming Facebook "friends" with other family members, and—the biggest surprise—forging connection with a group of women I had never known before.

Some of us had walked the medicine path of the shamans of the Q'ero people in Peru. Iva was a filmmaker who created the documentary *The Road to Q'eros: A Journey Home,* and had been invited to film ceremonies that had rarely, if ever, been photographed before. CC was a curandera living in New Mexico and holding *temazcal* ceremonies, sweat lodges in small domed structures. Teri was an acupuncturist steeped in the Eastern healing arts. Zelda was a drum-maker who created the Sacred Dream Circles, a series of seven-foot-tall metal framed dream catchers designed with intricate patterns weaving crystals in the web of each circle to heal ourselves and our Earth. Carla was a "cosmic crone" and had created the School of Womb Wisdom, teaching sovereignty in the realms of sex, wealth, and voice. Jane held prayer dances in Sound Peace Chambers, oval structures built to resonate sound inspired by a native elder, Joseph Rael. Mechelle was a registered nurse, Reiki master, sound therapist, and "angel communicator" at an Indian hospital in Arizona.

We would come to be known to people who connected with us online as *Sisters of the Lodge,* which was what we named our Facebook page. The idea was to create a virtual sacred space online in which we all could share in ceremonies, teachings, and traditions. Mayan prophecies were speaking of a time when Eagle, representing modern ways, would fly together with Condor, representing ancient wisdom. Our intention was to offer daily inspiration and ceremony from many traditions manifesting the prophecy of Eagle flying in the sky with Condor. Our Facebook page represented Eagle, the modern ways. Condor was the ancient ways represented by our ceremonies and teachings.

How exactly we came together—and how these powerful mystical connections happened—is beyond my knowledge, since it was the social media savvy of Carla Goddard that was responsible. I can't give you a guide on how to build a spiritual community with your Facebook page. What I do know is that Carla, the woman who started our page, had a vision—or, as she calls it, a "picture"—of Medicine Women gathering together to form a sacred circle, a circle that would build bridges between traditions to create a collective energy that would uplift and inspire. As our Facebook page puts it, *this circle of women is a divine orchestration of Spirit, and our connection is strong in synchronicity.*

And so it was.

Carla was extremely adept at social media. We all were able to elevate our individual pages by sharing each other's postings. Through collaboration, we could grow our Facebook presence in ways we never could do on our own. Our connections started online but would lead to in-person meetings over the years as we came to know each other better through our personal pages and postings.

Carla lived in Florida not far from my mom, so she and I had lunch at the sponge docks in Tarpon Springs when I visited. Our only previous connection was on Facebook, yet she seemed immediately familiar when we met. Having seen Carla's photos and read her postings, it felt as if I had known her before in some way. Soon after the excitement of our initial meeting settled, we discovered we would both be traveling at the same time. This may not seem like a miraculous occurrence, but for us, it sparked a vision for ceremony.

Carla was going to be at the Pacific in California while I would be on a family trip to the Atlantic. She was planning to take with her a prayer stick she had been gifted and release it to the ocean. I would be on a wild dolphin retreat with my family in Bimini, with a despacho ceremony planned while I was there. The idea for a bicoastal ceremony arose over lunch as our first virtual ceremony as *Sisters of the Lodge* was born between bites of gyros and forkfuls of Greek salad. Our intention was to allow the waters of the oceans to ceremonially cleanse us of whatever blocks the flow of joy in our lives. The ceremony would come to be called *Ascension to Joy*.

We used our Facebook page to bring the Ascension to Joy ceremony to life. An invitation was posted taking prayer requests online with the name of each participant added to the prayer stick in a daily ceremony by Carla. In the despacho ceremony, prayers are traditionally blown into coca leaves. Rather than coca leaves, prayers here would be blown into a natural sponge I had found at the docks the day Carla and I met. I posted a video on our Facebook page that participants could use to add their prayers for the ceremony.

I had learned about Joe Noonan, better known as the Dolphin Whisperer, through a mutual friend. Joe led people on adventure retreats to swim with wild dolphins. The idea of doing that became a quest from which I could not shake free. Somehow, I convinced my sisters that swimming with wild dolphins would be a once-in-a-lifetime experience for our families. Before long, we were in Fort Lauderdale boarding the smallest plane I had ever been on. A quick twenty-minute flight took me, my two sisters, and our six kids to Bimini.

The whole island could be seen from the window of our thirty-passenger plane as we flew over the Atlantic. Bimini is only seven miles long and two hundred yards wide. We landed on the tarmac outside the single-story concrete building that is the airport. A weathered blue wooden sign greeted us with the hand-painted words, *Thank you for flying to the Islands of the Bahamas.* The other greeting came from Joe, our dolphin whisperer who picked us up in a '69 VW bus. All of our luggage and all of our bodies were piled into the back. We drove just a few miles to our secluded weathered beach house with hammocks swinging between palm trees and white sand at our doorstep.

The natural beauty of Bimini was astonishing. Huge conch shells with polished pale pink interiors were strewn everywhere along the beaches. Coconuts heavy with milk hung low in the palm trees. Joe cracked them open with a machete, and we drank the clear milk out of natural shells. We were surrounded by warm turquoise waters, the calmest I had ever seen the Atlantic. Dolphins were in the forefront of our minds. They were the reason we had come.

Our *Ascension to Joy* ceremony was planned for the second day of the trip. It would also be our first day searching for dolphins. We drove to a nearby dock in what we now named the Magic Bus and boarded a power catamaran. With our captain, Kevin, at the helm and his wife, Kandy as first mate, we headed deeper and deeper into the ocean in search of dolphins. The boat had a broad flat bow in front which our teenage crew used for sunbathing. Joe and his son, Mark, would often jump into the ocean to spear fish which would later become our dinner. Riding along on the gentle waves with the broad and wide catamaran sailing close to the water was idyllic.

For the next four hours, on one of the calmest days on the ocean, not a single sign of dolphins could be found anywhere. Our hopes were deflated as Kevin steered the boat back toward shore. I was planning to hold the despacho ceremony on the shore near our beach house, as we would be there the same time Carla would be offering her prayers to the Pacific. Then we heard the word, the one we had been waiting for since we arrived.

"Dolphins," shouted Joe.

A few hundred feet from the boat, a fin appeared, an undeniable sign that yes, indeed there was a dolphin in our midst. The energy that had waned with the seeming end of our trip now surged with expectancy. In a few moments, fins were rising all around us. Silvery gray bodies leaped out of the ocean, gleaming against the sun. We were suddenly surrounded by dolphins. Seeing them was riveting. My heart suddenly felt as if it would burst from joy being so close to them. This, I realized, was it. This was the ceremony. This is what had been envisioned by two medicine women meeting for lunch just a few weeks earlier. *Ascension to Joy* was exactly what I was feeling.

The energy on the boat shifted as everyone began finding their gear and slipping into snorkels, fins, and masks. As I plunged underwater, reality transformed itself from a tangible earthly dimension to a fluid ethereal flow. The Atlantic, the ocean that had held me since birth, had never felt as sacred as in that moment when we wholeheartedly inhabited the home of these welcoming mammals. Noises were muted except for the echolocations of dolphins downloading frequencies of mystery. Having never been so close to dolphins, I was immediately struck by how their physicality has skillfully adapted them to a life in water, an element I was feeling completely inept in. Their entire body is streamlined for swimming, with every inch used to glide effortlessly through the water. Often, the synchronized motion they moved in seemed like dancing with each other in an underwater ballet. Their elongated mouths appeared to be in a perpetual smile. Being near them catapults a person to a state of joy.

We were truly blessed that day to swim with two pods of dolphins, often as many as fifteen to twenty at a time. Joe, our dolphin whisperer, said it was rare to have so many dolphins together at once. They stayed with us for an hour, but time that day felt both fleeting and eternal. As it came time to leave the watery world we had inhabited for a brief encounter with the wild and free dolphins of Bimini, we were cloaked in the power, beauty, and awe of the experience. We had been graced to enter this world for but a moment in time, and indeed had ascended to joy.

Once we returned to the beach house, I began preparing outside for the despacho. Although the traditional despacho originates high in the Andes of Peru, the despacho for our *Ascension to Joy* ceremony would align with the elements of the tropical island of Bimini. Rather than being held in wrapping paper, the despacho would be held in the sandy shores of the Atlantic. Instead of burning the despacho in a fire, water would be the element through which it would be offered to Spirit. I had brought a few items with me to Bimini for the ceremony. Along with the finger sponge from the docks at Tarpon Springs, I had packed a bag of Himalayan salt crystals, organic coca nibs to honor the lineage, and gold and silver resin to invoke masculine and feminine energies. I trusted that whatever else I might need would be there.

The despacho we created was a mandala in the sand. At the center sat the finger sponge holding the prayers of hundreds of souls who had joined our ceremony online. The sponge was set in a coconut shell and fed with coconut water, nourishing the prayers in its pure sweet nectar. A piece of rose coral found on the beach the day we arrived reminded me of an antenna, and was added to the sponge to amplify the signals of our intentions to the Universe.

The shamans had always taught us that the most important ingredient we bring to ceremony is our heart. The heartbeat of this despacho had been transformed by the wild beating hearts of the dolphins we swam with. The Himalayan salt crystals were sprinkled counterclockwise around the shell to energetically cleanse and unwind all that blocks the flow of joy in our hearts. Offerings of the coca nibs were placed in the coconut shell to honor the lineage of this ceremony from the Andes. Silver and gold resin were sprinkled around the shell to honor the sacred feminine and masculine of both Pachamama, the Earth, and Inti Ti-Ti, the Sun.

We dug a spiral in the sand circling out from the shell in concentric rings leading to the ocean. Colorful native flowers and small shells collected along the beach were added along this path as offerings. Two coconuts were placed at the north end, the top of the mandala despacho, to offer nourishment to our prayers. Joe had told us that coconut water was the purest water one can drink, as it is filtered through the trunks of the palm trees before being stored in the shell. It felt like divine sustenance for our ceremony.

Eleven of us were on retreat there, and each of us was represented by a conch shell. We blew personal prayers as well as prayers for our world into each shell, just as prayers in Peru would be blown into coca leaves. Once our prayers were offered, the conch shells were placed on the outer perimeter of our mandala despacho. I began circling around it in a clockwise direction building the energy of joy as I sang sounds and notes that seemed to come from Spirit, tones and melodies like nothing I had heard before. I am not a numerologist, but having eleven of us in that ceremony felt significant. In my most rudimentary understanding of numbers, it is easy to see the number one as the representation of Oneness. Its repetition amplifies its power. Eleven seemed to magnify the Unity Consciousness we had felt with the dolphins, the consciousness where all hearts meet as One and beat in Joy. Our mandala despacho sat in the sand until the tides came. All that remained the next morning after the sands had been washed clean were the eleven conch shells. It felt as if Spirit had left each of these for us as a gift, a tangible reminder of the magic and joy of the wild and free dolphins of Bimini.

Hundreds of people had joined online through comments on our Sisters of the Lodge page that were carried to both coasts, adding their prayers and their intention to be a part of this energetic web—me with a finger sponge to the Atlantic and Carla with a prayer stick to the Pacific. In our first ceremony as *Sisters of the Lodge*, Eagle and Condor surely flew together in magic and mystery. After leaving Bimini, my family returned to New York and I went back to Florida, where I'd been staying with my mom since leaving New York. A few weeks later, I would open an email that radically altered the trajectory of my life.

Ceremonies and rituals arise from many different traditions and paths. All have merit. All have value. There may be ceremonies and rituals that are already a part of your life. If not, you are free to make up any of your own. Ceremony and ritual honor who we are as sacred beings. Ceremony is the language of the soul. It elevates our language to the level of Spirit. We often think of ceremony as an elaborate event like a wedding or graduation with lots of time or money involved. But a ceremony can also be created to say thank you or ask for guidance or healing. It can be for the benefit of another person or for our planet. When we create a ceremony, we are calling on powers greater than our own and beyond our knowing to be of service. You don't need a certificate or special training to do this. Ceremony is the language of your soul. It deepens your connection to Spirit. Although the despacho ceremony comes to us from the shamans of the high Andes, what I loved about the Ascension to Joy despacho was that it so thoroughly reflected the elements of Bimini. I know I have taken many liberties with the despacho ceremony, but if you feel called to create a despacho ceremony, look around you. Discover elements from the land you live in to create ceremony with.

Another teaching from the shamans of Peru is that at the time of our birth, we are each held by a great power of nature. What mountain, ocean, or other large body of water held you when came into the world? Once I learned this, I knew right away that it was the Atlantic Ocean for me. The waves and sandy shores along

Smith Point Beach on the south shore of Long Island were the delight of my childhood. The shamans teach us that an honoring and acknowledgment of these places is needed to connect more deeply to the source of power that has kept watch over us. This ceremony was an honoring of one of the great loves of my life, the Atlantic Ocean.

CHAPTER EIGHTEEN

Truth or Consequences

I WAS BORN IN NEW York City and never lived more than fifty miles from its center. My roots felt deep, yet the seeds of departure had been germinating for years. There were financial concerns. The loss of child support for my older daughter was already leaving me precariously clinging to a rocky precipice where one financial slip could be ruinous. My younger daughter would turn eighteen the following year, meaning I would lose the help from Phil altogether. There was also an existential quest churning. I was looking for truth: truth about love, about purpose, about the meaning of life. I was afraid to feel the painful loss of Jon from my life after our breakup over the phone. My heart's deepest longing was to be near him again.

A few years before I left New York, Phil had remarried. He and his wife had recently bought a home together. When I told him I was leaving the city, he begged me not to go. Nothing or no one could have stopped me then. Although thoughts of leaving had been brewing in me for some time, to other people in my life, the decision seemed abrupt; they were stunned. I was practically free-floating at the thought of leaving. It would mean escape from the weight of a responsibility I didn't know I had been carrying until dreams not yet realized seemed to beckon on the horizon. I was desperate for a freedom that the life I was living had never offered. For the first time since our divorce, my daughters, now eighteen and nineteen, were living with their dad full time.

Phil and I had always lived within a few miles of each other. Sarabeth and Danielle spent a lot of time with their dad, but living with a parent full time is a different kind of relationship. With teenagers in your home, you try to keep track of their whereabouts, you wonder if you'll see them for dinner, you negotiate constantly about the car and what time they need to be home. As I look back on that monumental decision I made, I realize I was oblivious to anyone else's feelings in the matter. I didn't think about my daughters; I didn't think about my family; I didn't think about Phil. The upheaval in their lives would not have happened if I was not being driven by a compulsion to see Jon, one I could not even admit to myself since the dream to be with him again seemed so utterly unattainable. The fantasy lived in the lost caverns of my broken heart.

I gave my landlord notice and began packing up whatever I thought might be needed in a life I had not yet imagined. Anything too big, like my old TV cabinet, or too dangerous, like my chainsaws, were given away or left at the curb. (Why I had chainsaws remains a mystery.)

Among my possessions that seemed worthy of space in the Penske truck were suitcases of clothes for every season, the ten-speed bicycle Phil had bought me, a large floor rug from Anthropologie splattered with orange, red, and gray geometric patterns, a rollup futon mat, twenty years of memories crammed into photo albums and scrapbooks, a two-foot-tall selenite crystal lamp, a Champion juicer, a sheepskin mat, and a Tempur-Pedic mattress topper.

When I left New York I headed to Florida and stayed with my mom. The decision felt practical and seemed like the most realistic arrangement financially. The plan was to buy a home there with the little money I had left from selling my house on Long Island a few years earlier. Although my heart was in New Mexico, Florida was full of foreclosures and short sales at the time (although I'm still not sure what a short sale is). What I did know was that it was a good time to be a buyer. I spent a few months halfheartedly looking at real estate. Nothing in Florida made me feel like I wanted to live there or put down roots.

During those three months in Florida with my mom, a change in the course of my life flashed out of the empty air one day in the simple act of opening an email. It was a message no different from probably thousands just like it I had deleted over the years—from a recruiter looking for physical therapists. What caught my eye was the destination: Truth or Consequences, New Mexico. I had not been to New Mexico since my final visit with Jon, who was living there as a retired photographer. During my visits to Abiquiu, my love for him had taken root in the red rock landscape we explored together. I was intoxicated by the endless sky offering a barely perceivable taste of infinity. I was seduced by mountains which seemed to beckon with magic, just as the Andes had in Peru. When I envisioned moving to New Mexico to be with Jon, I could never imagine how it might be possible. The same thought would arise: "What do people do here?" I remember thinking, "I need to work." I could never imagine making a living in the remote rural communities of northern New Mexico.

Truth or Consequences! I never imagined such a place existed on earth. The name was speaking to my quest. Truth was what I was seeking, about so many things, most of it fueled by an unsettled longing since Jon had left my life. The quest to be with him felt beyond this lifetime, as if this was the latest wave in the tumultuous waters our karma had ridden before.

Many years earlier at Kripalu in the Berkshires, long before Jon had any thought of living in New Mexico, images that might have predicted my move came to me at a shamanic medicine training with Alberto Villoldo, founder of Four Winds. During our week-long retreat, we were often guided on shamanic journeys and soul retrievals transported by the steadfast beat of the drum. On one particular journey, I found myself taken to another era in time. Jon and I were together in what seemed like the late 1800s. I saw myself in a saloon wearing a tight corseted top and long hoop skirt. Small tables and chairs were scattered around a dusty room. A long bar ran the length of the back wall with bottles of liquor lining the shelves behind it. Men wearing derby-style caps and well-worn cowboy hats were sitting around drinking. I appeared to be working behind the bar wiping down the countertop. The scene could have been straight out of any of the Western shows I'd watched on TV growing up, or my first bartending job at the dive bar.

Jon walked into the saloon pushing his way through the two swinging doors. A shot was heard, and he fell face down on the dirt floor, shot from behind. I screamed as I ran toward him, and wept uncontrollably. He was the love of my life. Our relationship was perpetually dying a thousand deaths. It was as if our souls were always looking for a scenario that could unravel this karmic knot.

I followed up the recruiter's email and accepted a position with Sierra Health Care in Truth or Consequences, making home visits throughout southern New Mexico. T or C, as it is called, was four hours south of Jon in Abiquiu. I never told him I was moving.

One of the stranger things about this place with such a strange name was the old-time residents who insisted on calling the town by the name it had been formerly known as: Hot Springs. As a kid, I had watched the game show "Truth or Consequences" on TV. Once in T or C I found out that before it was on TV there was a radio version of the show. In 1950, the radio game show was celebrating its tenth anniversary. The host, Ralph Edwards, offered to broadcast the show from any city that was willing to change its name to Truth or Consequences. Hot Springs "won" (unless you're one of the old-timers).

It was a quirky town, with one Main Street full of funky boutiques, eclectic art galleries, the historic El Cortez old-time cinema, upscale food, and, of course, hot springs. Sid Bryan, my landlord, owned flamboyant rental properties and colorful spas that gave the dusty landscape a feel of whimsy. He rented efficiency-style apartments to out-of-towners or travelers like me. The rent included free soaks at his Pelican spas scattered around town. Spending thirty or forty minutes taking a hot soak in a private tub was by far the best part of living there.

Being a traveler for work allowed me to take baby steps in moving my life to New Mexico. Work contracts lasted three months. Each time mine came up for renewal, I would tell myself, "I can stay another three months." The baby steps went on for two years. Although New Mexico and New York stand next to each other on the alphabetical list of state names, New Mexico felt as far from the cosmopolitan center of the country as I could get. The only images I had ever seen of the American West were the ones I grew up watching on TV, and it wasn't at home but with my Aunt Eileen at my grandparents' bungalow. Episodes of "Gunsmoke," "Bonanza," and old John Wayne Westerns played on the old black-and-white TV set with a coat hanger for an antenna.

Now that I was living in New Mexico, the dry climate hit me in a way it never had done when I was visiting Jon from New York. Accustomed to the moisture and humidity in New York, I felt as if I was withering in the arid air. Every few hours, I needed Visine to keep my eyeballs from rubbing like sandpaper. Then there was the altitude, four thousand feet higher than the sea level I'd spent my whole life at. Every day in late afternoon, a deep fatigue enveloped me. At first, I thought stress was doing it from all the changes in my life, but when it lifted after about a month, I realized I had been adjusting to the intangible additive of altitude.

Learning to navigate the remote rural terrain of New Mexico may end up being one of my life's greatest accomplishments. My territory included a hundred-mile radius heading west to Winston, north to Monticello, and south to Hatch. Directions from the office to patient visits would often read: "Turn right off the county road. When you see a large cottonwood, cross over the cattle guard and follow the arroyo. Once you pass the old sawmill, look to the right for a tan double-wide." Coming from New York, I had no idea what any of these landmarks were. I began second-guessing my decision to move to New Mexico. After a lifetime of navigating an urban grid where GPS could find any address, the rugged open landscape left me feeling I'd gotten in way over my head. How would I find patients living in homes without numbers along dirt roads without names?

One of the most endearing customs of this part of the country was discovered while driving along the lone highways, country roads and dirt lanes. Drivers would wave as we passed each other—not a full-fledged back-and-forth of the wrist and hand but a uniquely New Mexican wave, with thumb wrapped around the wheel and the other four fingers straight up at attention. I found myself reflexively responding in the same way. I imagine to people living in New Mexico this custom was never contemplated, as it appeared so woven into the folklore of the culture.

Coming from New York where nobody waved to anybody, I was charmed by the phenomenon. I remember mentioning it to a patient who told me she had wondered the same thing when she was little. She asked her father, "Do you know that person?"

"No," he'd said of the passing driver he waved to. "But it lets you know that someone has an eye on you. Someone sees you in case you're ever in trouble out here." That's what it felt like. In this vast open space and endless sky, someone had, in fact, seen me.

The endless acres of crops stunned me as I drove to remote home visits throughout southern New Mexico. The climate is unforgiving, water is scarce, the sun brutal, and the spring winds relentless. I remember thinking, "Anyone who gets anything to grow here is a genius!" Miraculously, the flat fertile lands were full of corn and hay, apples and apricots, livestock and the cash crop of New Mexico: green chile. Hatch, about forty miles south of T or C, was the capital of the chile universe and was part of my territory. Every year, the Chile Festival takes over for Labor Day weekend, and green chiles are found roasting everywhere, tumbling around in large barrel-shaped cages outside markets and groceries. There was no escaping the late summer perfume of smoky sweetness that permeated the air. Large burlap sacks of green chiles filled every home where they would be roasted in ovens and outdoor grills.

My first chile relleno came from the kitchen of a patient in Hatch. The smell of roasting chiles filled the house as I entered for a patient visit. Before I left, his wife insisted I take a chile relleno. First, she had roasted the chile and cleaned out the seeds, then made a slit and inserted a stick of *queso*, the Mexican white cheese. After that, she dipped the chile in an egg white batter, dropped it into a flour mixture, fried it on the stove until the chile was lightly browned, then wrapped it all in a homemade tortilla warm from the griddle. Take it for the road, she insisted. As I bit into the soft tortilla, the melted cheese oozed through the sweet and smoky spice of the green chile. I had never tasted anything so exquisitely luscious. In the many times I've ordered chile rellenos since then, none have measured up to the heavenly experience from that humble home in Hatch.

Beyond the climate, the altitude, the unaccustomed customs, and the green chiles, it was the remarkable resourcefulness of the people that astounded me most of all. The rugged landscape seemed to carve those who lived here into brilliant pioneers stretching the scarcest of resources into gold. From mud and straw, adobe bricks made by hand were shaped into homes by the many families I met.

Upon learning that someone had built their own home I would ask in astonishment, "How do you know how to build a house?"

"You just do it!" they would say matter-of-factly with a look that seemed to ask, "How do you not know how to build a house?" If you needed help with your home in New York, you picked up the phone and called a carpenter, electrician, or plumber. If you needed help in New Mexico, you called a neighbor. I heard countless stories of families teaching their children to make adobe bricks for rooms to build onto their homes, which often accounted for the patchwork layout in the homes I visited.

Many people in outlying communities beyond T or C had no computers or access to the internet. A telepathic rural network took its place. Patients would often be the ones to let me know whom I would be seeing for physical therapy before I ever got a referral from my agency. They knew everything that was going on in their communities. So-and-so had a stroke, or this one was in a car accident. "You'll be seeing them soon for therapy," they would tell me.

It was through this rural network that I learned the story of a twenty-year-old woman who had been paralyzed in a car accident. She lived in Monticello, a remote rural town of about a hundred fifty people with expansive views that took my breath away. She had swerved to avoid a deer and overcorrected, toppling upside down into a ditch along the highway. A spinal cord injury paralyzed her from the waist down, her life forever altered. The youngest of her three children was nineteen months old. As I drove the twenty-five miles from T or C to see her for the first time, I braced myself for the worst. I never imagined that the young woman I would meet in a wheelchair would teach me what it meant to be a warrior. I couldn't find one shred of self-pity or anger. She was a beacon of positivity and one of the most spirited people I've ever met. She just figured she would have to learn new ways to do things, and that was that. I wished there was some way to bottle her magical superpowers so that others could drink from the wellspring of her strength.

As I was adjusting to a new land and a new job, I had decided not to tell Jon I was in New Mexico. I wanted my life to land on some solid ground before contacting him. I had no idea what he would think. I thought for sure he would think I was some kind of crazed stalker. During this extreme transition, work was my salvation. Helping others whose needs were far greater than my own lifted me out of my fears and insecurities. One such instance of my salvation was a woman on hospice who had been bedridden for nearly a year. There is a lot to learn from someone for whom death is so near. The work my patient and I were doing together was to get her on her feet so she could stay in her home to die—an insurance company requirement to cover her hospice care. This work took all of our focus. The woman was much larger than me; her legs were not always under her control; one missed step and she would be down, with no way of getting back up. I followed here intently as she walked with her walker, holding her with one hand as my other pulled her wheelchair behind her.

When we first started working together, she could manage only a few shaky steps. But after a few weeks, to my surprise, she was doing remarkably well and could push her walker for short distances in her home. One day, we ventured to the back of the house, a space she had not been in for nearly a year. After ten feet, she sat back in her wheelchair as magical tones filled the air. "Where did that beautiful sound come from?" I wondered. Then I glanced around and saw three Koshi chimes gently swinging in an archway where my head had inadvertently hit them as we passed underneath.

I had only discovered Koshi chimes a few months earlier. Tito La Rosa, an Andean musician and sound healer from Peru was a featured performer at YogaSource, a popular yoga studio in Santa Fe. Using a variety of flutes, rattles, strings and other instruments I had never seen, he created ceremony through the frequency of sound. His ethereal music was soul stirring and healing. I had traveled to Santa Fe to partake in the ceremony. As the workshop was nearing its end we were instructed to lie on our backs. Tito walked the room gently swinging Koshi chimes bathing us in their gentle tones. I was captivated by their sound and ordered them online once I returned home.

"I love Koshi chimes," I told her.

"You can have them," she said.

My impulse was to refuse. "Oh no, I can't," I told her. I was sure there was an unwritten rule somewhere about not taking gifts from patients, especially those so close to death.

"I see how your eyes light up when you look at them," the woman said. "I'd much rather you enjoy them now; otherwise, they're going to end up in some yard sale once I'm gone. It's much more fun this way."
I enter someone's home as a teacher of sorts, to help them navigate a crisis. My role as teacher is not a permanent perch. Often, I find I am the student. This woman whose death was near was teaching

me now. Not only did my refusal of her gift shut down my own delight but I was also denying her the pleasure of giving them to me. Once I could see the reciprocity in both giving and receiving for us both, I left her home feeling like a child on Christmas morning, holding one of the purest gifts I have ever received.

Perhaps no one defined the pioneering spirit of New Mexico more than Bonnie, a woman born in 1928. I was seeing her because of difficulties with balance. As I entered her home, I was struck by a photo on a round wooden table draped in lace-trimmed cloth in a corner of the living room. It was her, Bonnie wanted me to know, in the eight-by-ten black-and-white photograph, at twenty years old. I never would have recognized the frail woman in front of me wearing a wig and housecoat as the timeless beauty in the frame. In the photograph, a young woman was looking back over her shoulder. Long, dark curly hair ran down her back. Her lips were full and slightly parted. Even though the photo was black-and-white, you could tell that her lips were painted a deep color.

"Absolutely stunning!" I told her as she held up the photo.

"I was a local beauty queen winner," she said proudly. Her parents had never let her leave their little Texas town to pursue a beauty career such as modeling, but Bonnie had bigger dreams to follow.

On one visit, I guided her into a half moon yoga pose, stretching her spine while supported against the wall. She said it reminded her "of the tricks I used to do on my skates." In southern New Mexico, I asked, "Where did you find ice for skating?"

"Oh no, I didn't skate on ice. I used wheels. There were two things I wanted to do in my life," Bonnie said matter-of-factly. "One was skating. The other was flying planes."

"Flying planes?" I asked incredulously. "Who taught you how to fly a plane?"

"My husband bought a plane, and I just taught myself," she said. After buying a second plane, she told me, she and her husband used them to deliver newspapers to ranchers in southern New Mexico by dropping them out of the plane in bundles. It was an intimate glimpse into the pioneer living inside this woman who now wobbled as she walked.

As much as I loved the rural communities, the quirky downtown, and the soothing hot springs of Truth or Consequences, my heart was up north where Jon lived. I waited a few months to let him know I had moved to New Mexico.

I wanted some ground under my feet as I settled into a new place, a new routine, a whole new way of life. I knew that if I were to live in New Mexico I could not revolve my life around Jon. Adjusting to the altitude took about a month. It took about another seven months to send Jon an email to let him know I had moved.

He replied:

Hi Karen,
I can't believe you have moved to New Mexico. Where are you living? Hope you have your long underwear. I look forward to hearing about your journey.

I never could have configured the steps that were guiding me to a life so foreign to anything I had ever known. It was as if the same force that was driving my desire to kiss Jon was now uprooting my life in every way imaginable. Moving to New Mexico felt like the biggest gamble I had ever made. The old guideposts were gone, replaced by a life of uncertainty. My work was truly my salvation. Serving others whose needs were far greater than my own is what lifted me up.

You do not have to turn your life upside down in order to feel overwhelmed. Life can easily trigger our fears and worry. It comes all too easily from the anxieties of every-day life, the stresses of family, job, home, friends, health. The list goes on and on. Serving another can truly be the way to save yourself, to assist in loosening the vice grip these emotions can bind us in.

In Native American cultures, there is the tradition of the Giveaway, often a ceremony, in which the guests receive a valued gift, with nothing expected in return. The chimes from my hospice patient were a Giveaway in its purest form. (Giving away clothes you no longer wear is not in this spirit.) What might you possess that you know someone else would treasure?

A Giveaway does not need to be in material form, an object. Your greatest possession is your heart, your most valuable resource is your time. Is there someone who would benefit from the gift of your company? A neighbor or friend you can reach out to and offer your service in some way? Where can a random act of kindness bring joy? Does a person in your life not know how much you appreciate them? Is there someone you are holding bitterness, anger, or resentment toward? Can you give that away to right a relationship, to say, *I'm sorry*, or *Please forgive me?* Can you comfort someone with the words *I love you* without needing to hear them in return? In serving others in this way, we can receive so much more than we give.

CHAPTER NINETEEN

Cavedigger

IT WOULD BE ANOTHER FEW months before I would actually see Jon again. We were living about two hundred fifty miles apart, a four-hour drive. By this time, he was also seeing another woman. Emails were our method of communicating until finally we made a plan to meet again. My message said:

> *I do hope my heart has the strength to see you without breaking, Jon. I do not expect you to have any understanding of the devastation after our breakup. It has been a long recovery, one that has brought me back to the scene of the crime. Close but not too close. Plus I like the name, Truth or Consequences.*

Once again, we would be back together in Abiquiu, the place I had last seen Jon, a place that both enchanted and haunted me. I was terrified to see him again, yet the longing was like nothing I had ever known. It had propelled me to pull up the deep roots of my citified life and replace them in T or C with one that was unrecognizable, devoid of any scent of familiarity to cling to. Jon was the reason I had come.

What was it like to finally be together with him again? All recollection of our reunion has been obliterated—by the fear and uncertainty I was feeling at once again seeing the man who had rejected me but lived on in my heart. The weight of every unalterable decision and every unrequited desire, of an utterly unknown future, penetrated each moment with him during our reunion. I was overwhelmed. Even now, I have no memory of that time other than this note he wrote to me:

> *Your brave visit was a testament to the woman I loved and respected, a woman who walks through this world with compassion and wisdom. When we embraced, saying goodbye, I felt your heart. It was so loud and fast. It was pounding against your chest. I felt all your love for me. Your heart felt so vulnerable, so raw, so open. I felt the woman I loved; your tenderness, your dedication, your support. I think about how brave you were in coming here. I think about how difficult being in relationship is for me. I thank you for opening your trembling heart and letting me feel all of you once again.*

Reading this, I knew there was something between us that felt solid and meaningful. Maybe I had not come all this distance in my life just chasing some crazy delusion. Maybe there was something that was real. Maybe I wasn't crazy after all.

Despite uprooting my life thousands of miles from anything I had ever known, miraculous networks were arising in New Mexico. Arms and hearts felt as if they were reaching out to welcome me in this unfamiliar land. The web of connections was serendipitous steps that would ultimately usher me to the life I had been afraid to envision when I left New York.

I met Falcon Black Feather at a Gathering of Healers organized by my Lodge sister, Mechelle, who worked on the Navajo reservation in Fort Defiance, Arizona. The Gathering was a three-day event to heal the healers and replenish the soul, full of ceremony, music, food, and laughter. Many of the Lodge sisters from our Facebook group were there.

Falcon was a Native American blues musician from Santa Fe, tall and lean with a long black ponytail hanging down from under a flat-top gaucho hat. He wore small round glasses over soulful eyes which looked as if they had seen many, many lifetimes. An easy kinship developed between Falcon and me over that weekend. A few weeks later, I would be listening to him playing blues guitar in a cave in Embudo.

The cave was carved by Ra Paulette, known as the Cavedigger. Using only hand tools, Ra carves underground temples deep in the Earth throughout the rugged hills of Northern New Mexico. These works of Earthen Art begin by hauling endless wheelbarrows of dirt out of the ground. What begins as a humble tunnel transforms into soaring cathedrals underground with walls smooth as alabaster. Altars and staircases, balconies and shrines become masterfully etched into these monumental works of art by the hands of one man.

Embudo is a small community nestled in the stunning hillsides along the Rio Grande. Going to hear Falcon, I drove slowly along the rough, jagged dirt road leading to the home of Steve and Tyler, whose property the cave was on. After parking, I followed a short trail hugging the hill to a small plywood door. Behind it, the hand-carved cave of Ra Paulette was extraordinary.

Stepping underground gave me a deep sense of being held by the Mother. It is hard to imagine how dirt could be shaped into smooth white surfaces with patterns and motifs carved into them. Small built-in seats and altar spaces were meticulously carved into the curving walls. A staircase spiraled up to a balcony leading to a second floor. The childlike delight and wonder of being in such a magical space filled me with awe and reverence. Being in the belly of our Earth Mother held me in places that had been abandoned for so long I'd forgotten the deep ache to be held. The desire to hold ceremony here was profound, but in truth, no ceremony was needed. Entering the sacred underground cathedral was ceremony itself.

Yet I had in mind a gathering there that would transport people and transcend the framework of their everyday lives by bringing them together in a ceremonial way. Falcon would later put me in contact with Steve and Tyler. I asked Steve if the cave might be available for this, and he agreed. I am still humbled at the trusting generosity of Steve and Tyler, who allowed a woman they had never met to bring a group of strangers to their property to hold a ceremony in a mystical cave on their land.

At the heart of ceremony was building a despacho, an offering to Mother Earth, to Spirit, and to our ancestors. The first ceremony would take place Easter weekend. It is a time in northern New Mexico when tens of thousands of Catholics from all over the world make an annual pilgrimage to the Santuario de Chimayó, an adobe church in the heart of the old village. Good Friday walkers, some from far away, converge there along local highways and roads. Crosses carried by some symbolize the one Jesus carried to the crucifixion. At the Santuario, they light candles and offer prayers, but the true destination is the healing dirt in the tiny chapel next to it. There, pilgrims can lay their feet in the dirt, which is revered for its ability to heal. For over a hundred years, these walkers have come infusing the land with their faith. It felt like a powerful time to have our first ceremony at the cave.

Invitations went out online. Preparations began about a month before the ceremony. Getting the cave ready involved a five-hour drive north from Truth or Consequences to Embudo. I arrived there with a broom, a shovel, and a bucket. I often think this is how most ceremonies start: by clearing and cleaning space. The cave was no different. Its smooth, plaster-like surface was hard to believe, but even there, it was impossible to escape the dust in New Mexico. It had crept into every crevice and left a film everywhere. Cleaning and clearing the space was the first step. Once layers of dust were removed, tall red glass candles were placed around the cathedral-like cave to be lit before the ceremony.

It had been nearly a year since Jon and I reunited. Spending time together was challenging. We were living four hours apart. Jon had also been in another relationship. We kept in touch through emails. Before I began heading to Embudo to prepare for ceremony his other relationship ended. That meant I was able to stay at his house while preparing the cave for the ceremony. Spending weekends together rekindled our relationship as lovers, though the many miles between us kept any real intimacy at a distance. Jon became a ceremonial partner, helping to tend to the caves while providing space for me to land. Stepping into ceremony came so naturally to him. He was a Divine Masculine counterpart whose support was immeasurable.

Easter weekend arrived. A small group of travelers drove the rough off-road mile to Steve and Tyler's land, then hiked along the hillside to the humble wooden door. One could easily overlook the plywood entrance and never know the miraculous phenomenon of the cave within. Eleven women and two men passed through the gateway for our first ceremony in the underground hand-carved temple.

Everyone took a bit of time to walk the space in wonder. Awe enveloped us. We then gathered in a circle at the center of the cave, with a skylight overhead letting the early afternoon light fill the space. The candles glowed red against the alabaster walls curving around the labyrinthine space. Brief introductions were made. The miraculous source that had guided each of us to a mystical cave in northern New Mexico was palpable. Heart connections were forged by the ease with which gratitude and love was shared amongst former strangers. Nearly everyone was from New Mexico. One couple from Canada happened to be traveling in New Mexico at the time of the ceremony.

The despacho was at the heart of our gathering. We prepared for the ceremony with simple yoga postures and breath, drumming and silence, meditation and stillness held in the womb of the Mother. Then we moved outside for our despacho. Despite any liberties I may take in translating the centuries-old ceremony of the Andes, the essence of the heart's connection with the Earth is unchanged. Rather than the Peruvian tradition of covering our prayers and offerings in wrapping paper, we dug a shallow hole in the sandy soil with our hands and buried our prayers. Pachamama, the goddess mother of the Earth, held our hearts and prayers, our gratitude and longings. I felt so grateful at the way this humble idea had come together and manifested into joyous strangers connecting in such a palpable love.

Two months later, using that mystical cave and another nearby, we would hold a women's retreat and ceremony at the summer solstice to *Embody the Sacred Temple of Our Womb.* The caves offered rich inspiration for the ceremony, as the space itself compelled a deep communion with our Earth Mother, Pachamama. The despacho we created would honor the *Wild and Untamed Divine Feminine.* This time, we adorned a loaf of sweet challah bread with roses, wild flowers, and fresh eucalyptus.

The ceremonial offering was a work of art that truly embodied the wild and untamed souls of all the women who were there. We walked the half-mile to the river and offered the despacho to the flowing waters. Ceremony in my life has become a channel to Spirit, a line of communication for prayers and intentions to travel along. An attachment to outcome must be released with any ceremony or else it is simply an exercise for our mind. Ceremony has often brought devastation to my life, but within the upheaval, blessings were disguised.

The despachos in the caves of Ra Paulette were no different. A few short months after the ceremonies, my life would once again be upended.

Co-creating with Spirit attracts opportunities that you could not have invoked on your own. You tap into a synchronistic realm that is beyond reason, and possibilities exist where none was there before. Obstacles are lifted, pathways created. The less your intention is burdened with your own personal agenda and direction, the greater the power of Spirit to work through you. If certainty, fact, and logic have been the tools you've used to navigate your life, conscious co-creation with Spirit will challenge the foundation on which you have built your beliefs.

Cultivating a relationship with Spirit is not a one-way path in which you ask for what you want and all is provided. As with every relationship, it calls for reciprocity and mutual exchange. For your part, you are called to shed many things that have gotten in the way of this conscious creative process. You are asked to let go of expectations, let go of how you think things should be, let go of the idea that you have control over events or people in your life. You are asked to stop blaming others for your own unhappiness. You are asked to step into the flow of mystery, and are challenged to become comfortable with not-knowing. In this process of conscious co-creation, you are asked to cultivate faith and trust, to fortify your confidence in your spiritual self. When you begin to trust your higher self, you come to know the ways of magic. As you set an intention, obstacles to that intention must die through means such as ceremony or writing. This great cycle of life and death is what moves us through the time and space of our lives. The largest cycle occurs between your first inhalation as you enter the world and your last exhalation as you leave it. Yet within this large circle of your life-and-death cycle occur many small cycles of varying degrees and intensities.

Within these, take some time to ask what you would like to create in your life. What would you like to receive from or call into your life? Where would you like to create change? Are there issues that weigh heavily on you and cause distress? What would you like to step into? To set an intention, you can begin by listing the things in your life that you feel are not working, areas where you feel stuck, places that feel as if they will never change.

Notice what is causing the most distress for you. You may be unhappy with your work life. You may feel a lack of purpose or meaning. You may have fear around a lack of money or other resources. Perhaps you live with chronic pain or are facing a health crisis. Do relationships cause you stress? As you call to mind an aspect of your life that brings distress, close your eyes and notice how this feels in your body. Can you sense any areas that are tight or clenching? Do you feel anxious or uneasy? Are there places in your body that feel as if they are holding on or gripping? What does your overall mental and emotional state feel like?

Now, imagine what it would feel like if you were living without this distress. With eyes closed, notice how this feels in your body. Can you sense any subtle shifts in how your body feels as you move from thinking about the distress to imagining your life without it?

From the insights of this practice, notice what you would like to receive. What would you like to create? Who are you ready to step into becoming? What parts of yourself are you ready to reclaim? How do you want to walk through your life? What is the essence of what you are seeking?

See if you can distill the essence of your intention into one or two words. Once you have an intention, you can empower it with ceremony. A very simple way to begin working with Spirit and the elements is with a stone. Find two stones. These may already be in your possession or come from the land where you live. With the first stone, you will use your exhale to blow into it all of the distressing thoughts and feelings you noticed in the first practice. Continue exhaling until you have a sense of completion. This stone will be released in Nature either in the earth or in a natural body of water. Then, you will exhale into your second stone the intention that was distilled into a word or two. Exhale into the stone the thoughts and feelings you noticed as you imagined your life without the distress. You can keep this stone on an altar or sleep with it under your pillow or use it in any way you may feel called to. You may choose to release this stone at some point as well. Allow your intuition to guide you.

CHAPTER TWENTY

A Dream Come True

THE TRAVEL POSITION I HAD taken in Truth or Consequences allowed me to take baby steps along the road to belonging in New Mexico. The three-month contracts turned into two years until all the baby steps trampled beneath my feet. After twenty-one months and seven contracts, I returned to New York for a month in August, about a month after the women's retreat in the cave. My two sisters and I began making plans for a Thanksgiving visit they would make to New Mexico. This was not to be in T or C where I lived but at a large airbnb with an adjacent sauna that I rented for the occasion in Abiquiu. I wanted my family to experience the part of New Mexico I had fallen in love with, and that was up north.

During my time in New York, I attended a five-day silent meditation retreat at a humble zendo on the North Shore of Long Island. I have sat on silent meditation retreats before, but this one was different. For no reason at all, many moments were striking me as completely absurd. Sitting on my cushion, it was all I could do to keep from bursting out laughing. Since this was a silent retreat, containing my laughter was even more challenging. I could not make sense of my inappropriate urge to laugh, and I asked the roshi, or teacher, about zen's take on laughing. I was afraid of being reprimanded for not being a good meditator or not taking the retreat seriously enough. Instead, he shared with me this poem by Lisel Mueller:

The Laughter of Women

The laughter of women sets fire
to the Halls of Injustice
and the false evidence burns
to a beautiful white lightness

It rattles the Chambers of Congress
and forces the windows wide open
so the fatuous speeches can fly out

The laughter of women wipes the mist
from the spectacles of the old;
it infects them with a happy flu
and they laugh as if they were young again

Prisoners held in underground cells
imagine that they see daylight
when they remember the laughter of women

It runs across water that divides,
and reconciles two unfriendly shores
like flares that signal the news to each other
What a language it is, the laughter of women,
high-flying and subversive.
Long before law and scripture
we heard the laughter
we understood freedom.

I felt a new vigor as I returned to T or C, restored and renewed after my time in New York. Plans were in place for my family to visit in a few months. Life was falling into a satisfying rhythm. For the first time in my life, I had a sense of being capable of taking care of myself financially, fulfilling the vow I had made to myself at eight years old.

Then, in the sudden way that life can instantly change direction, my transition back to T or C turned out far more ominous than I could have expected. My landlord, Sid, had rented my spacious and airy one-bedroom apartment to someone else, leaving me with little option but an efficiency-style apartment along a short strip of apartments he owned downtown. It was a dark and spare studio with no stove and a sombrero hanging on the wall as art. It was a major disappointment compared with my previous light-filled apartment up on a hill.

Six weeks into my eighth travel contract—nearly two years of working and living in T or C—I got a call from the Arizona office of the recruiting company that had hired me. "We are getting a lot of calls from the supervisor there," I was told. "A lot of patients are calling with complaints about you."

I had never heard anything about this. "What kind of complaints?" I asked.

"We are not at liberty to say. We are terminating your contract at the end of the week," said the voice at the other end of the line. I wasn't even sure who I was talking to. My head was spinning. I couldn't make sense of what she was saying. I tried to find out more, but the call went dead.

I was being fired. I had never been fired. I was terrified and humiliated and confused. I may have many flaws as a woman, a wife, a mother, and a lover, but my work as a physical therapist was something I was proud of. I had a wealth of experience gathered through decades of tending to injuries, illnesses, and pain. Although I see a patient for a physical problem they are having, the countless stories of trauma I have listened to allowed me to see things from a holistic point of view. Our thoughts, feelings and family history all land in our body in some way shape or form. Sometimes gentle coaxing was needed for someone to see how their critical self-talk was an obstacle to their recovery or where loving attention was needed for healing. When I left someone's home I often felt the space had been uplifted in some way. Through my work, I found a deeper well of compassion and a set of skills that allowed me to be of service in the world. It was the one place in my life that gave me a sense of value and worth. If I was nothing else, I was good at my work. (I learned later that two new graduates, a husband and wife, had been hired to replace me.)

None of this made sense. My supervisor at Sierra Health Care was surprised that I'd been fired and said he had not received any complaints. No one at the corporate office would take my calls. The recruiter who'd gotten me the job in the first place had nothing to offer other than work in other states. It wasn't just the humiliation of being fired that was devastating but also the fact that I felt I was being lied to. I was awash in shame as I tried to figure out what to do. I couldn't afford to be without a job. I was terrified. I remember returning to the efficiency apartment where I threw myself on the strange bed with the stiff mattress, sobbing until my eyes turned red and puffy. I had been priced out of living in New York. The cost of living in the place where I was born, the place where I grew up and raised my family was no longer affordable. Returning to New York was not an option. I was alone and isolated in a remote part of the country where jobs were limited. I had only a few weeks before I would need to move out. Being fired—and lied to—by the office that had hired me made me vow never to work with a recruiter again.

I headed north that weekend to see Jon in Abiquiu. Passing through Española, the sign for Presbyterian Hospital on Paseo de Oñate seemed to beckon in a way I'd never noticed before. On a whim, I turned left into the entrance. A small one-story building stood next to the hospital with a sign that said Home Care on it. I parked the car, hit the buzzer at the entrance and the receptionist at the front desk let me in. I told her I was a physical therapist and was looking for a job. "Let me get our supervisor," she replied. A few moments later, a woman a bit older than me with short hair, glasses, and a warm smile ushered me to a seat in her office.

I told her I was a physical therapist. "I do home visits," I said, "and wonder if you're looking for someone."

"Well, the woman who has that job is retiring in three weeks," she told me.

My mind was racing as the words tumbled through my brain. Retiring? Three weeks? Did I get that right?

"Presbyterian is a highly professional organization," the woman said. She was referring to my appearance. I was not planning to look for a job that day and had walked into the office wearing jeans, moccasin ankle boots, and a brown suede fringe jacket cropped at the waist. My hair, which is naturally curly, was hanging loose, long, and free. I was not the picture of professionalism walking into the building that day.

"We would need to get you set up for an interview but you have to do something with your hair," was her advice to me.

After a whirlwind weekend, I returned to T or C. Within two days, the woman I'd met in the Home Care office called to schedule an interview. I was stunned at how quickly things were moving. After that initial interview and two more that followed, I was offered a job as a home care physical therapist. I was awestruck at the miracle that had landed in my lap.

Working up north meant I also needed to find a place to live. Although Jon and I were back in each other's lives, living together was not something either of us wanted. A friend sent me a Craigslist ad for a casita rental in Abiquiu, and I asked Jon if he could check it out for me. It was less than three miles from his home. He met the landlord, stepped inside, and said, "She'll take it." He was an anchor of steadfast kindness as I struggled to make sense of the turbulence breaking my life apart. The gratitude I felt toward Jon was immeasurable.

Out of the 121,697 square miles that make up the state of New Mexico, I was now living less than three of those miles away from Jon.

As my life in T or C crumbled, everything I needed to live in Abiquiu was laid before me. I had manipulated our first kiss, but living around the corner from Jon in the vast state of New Mexico was beyond anything I could have willed into existence by any earthly means. I often said to people during that time that it felt as if the Red Sea was parting. I was riding a mystical ship carrying me to a life I was afraid to dream of, for I never imagined it could come true. I was soaring through the land of enchantment where every wish that had lived in my heart since my first visit with Jon in New Mexico was being fulfilled.

I emptied the storage unit on the outskirts of T or C that held the mismatched pieces of furniture and assorted odds and ends of my life. My lodge sister who sent the Craigslist ad also sent her former husband Mike to meet me with a pick-up. Everything was piled into the back of his truck. He followed me up to Abiquiu, where we put it all in Jon's truck for the winding trip to my new home and the more-detailed task of actually moving in.

I followed him along a county road around the corner from where he lived. The road divided the land between property along the Rio Chama and land up on the mesa. As we turned left along a long dirt driveway to the mesa top, I realized I had been on this road before. Jon and I had driven this same road on my last visit with him before I left New York. The casita I was moving into was a stone's throw from a square two-story house that was also the studio of an artist whom Jon and I had visited on the annual Abiquiu Studio Tour a few years earlier. I remembered taking pictures of his home, fascinated by the stone-and-adobe structure seeming to rise out of the Earth, so unlike the suburban houses and concrete towers I was used to in New York. Large wooden planks extending in from the adobe walls created a precarious staircase to the second-floor bedroom. Outside, those same planks extending through the wall led to a small balcony off the bedroom.

The stone casita I was renting sat across from the studio on a patch of scrub and sandy soil high enough on the mesa so that from my back porch, I could see Pedernal, the defining flat-topped mountain that enthralled Georgia O'Keeffe when she lived and worked in Abiquiu. Another woman was living next door to me in the main stone home, but despite our close proximity, the space felt private.

My most mystical neighbor turned out to be a German shepherd named Snoopy who was living wild and free on the mesa although she had once belonged to someone nearby. Before I moved to New Mexico, the only dogs I knew lived in fenced yards and walked on leashes. Snoopy was the first dog I ever met who fully embodied her true dog nature. With the dark brown fur and black eyes of a shepherd, Snoopy looked intimidating to anyone who didn't know her. But for those of us living on the mesa, she was our queen, regal and majestic. Snoopy seemed to live in two worlds, the outside one where she roamed free and the one in the homes of our small community which she relied on for food, water, and occasional mobile vet visits.

Snoopy did not like feeling trapped in the confines of a house for more than a few minutes, and was never fully domesticated. The first time Snoopy stepped into my casita felt like a blessing, as if I had gained her trust. She didn't stay long. Her wild, free spirit always drew her to the mesa's rolling hills and dry arroyos, the shade of the juniper trees, and the vast night sky. She seemed to appoint herself as guardian of our little community. I remember hearing her barking outside one winter night with the snow blowing and the winds howling. It must have been two or three in the morning. I tried coaxing her inside but she took one look at me and ran off barking into the night, called by the distant howl of coyotes. Snoopy truly embodied the Buddhist teachings of non-attachment. She loved fiercely but was attached to no one. Her closest companion was Daisy, a tall, tan, skinny dog who ran the mesa with her despite having a dependable owner and a place to call home for the night.

About a week after I moved in, I read a Facebook post from my friend Steve in Embudo.

Some dirt bag dumped three puppies on our road. They wandered down confused, crying, and howling. Our neighbor found them and is giving them love, food, and shelter. I wish I had seen the person that dropped them off. So angry! If anyone awesome needs a super sweet puppy, these sure could use some love and a good home.

I told Jon, who was the ultimate dog lover and looking for a dog, about the post. He wasn't interested in a puppy. Neither was I, but I couldn't shake the thought of those abandoned pups. I was talking about this puppy with a highly intuitive friend of mine from T or C who told me, "I think that puppy is for you."

I had no idea of ever having a dog again, no less a puppy. I had just moved into a new place. I was getting ready to start a new job. A puppy did not seem to fit the picture of this new life ahead of me. I decided to head to Dixon to meet the puppies anyway.

When I went to their temporary home at the Dixon Animal Protection Society, the three little bundles of tan and white fur were wrapped around each other. One immediately tumbled off the others and ran straight to my lap, licking me incessantly. How could I say no? I left Dixon with a new puppy. His body hung low to the ground on stubby little legs. His ears flopped over and his eager black eyes never stopped looking at me. Most likely, he was a mix of corgi and Jack Russell terrier. I named him Jethro after one of my favorite rock bands of the '70s, Jethro Tull. Having seen Snoopy and Daisy living a life of freedom on the mesa, I decided this would be Jethro's world too.

When Snoopy and Daisy were around, I opened the front door to let Jethro play with the big dogs on the mesa. He was excited to have playmates, but from my perspective, it looked like he was being bullied by the older dogs. They wrestled him to the ground, pinned him down, and grabbed him by the neck, all the while growling fiercely. Every day started anew with Jethro eager to play, forgetting that he had been browbeaten the day before. Every day, Jethro would once again be overpowered by Snoopy and Daisy. Although my initial impulse was to try to save him from being hurt, what I came to see was that the big dogs on the mesa had a lot to teach Jethro about where he belonged. He was a puppy. He had a certain position in the hierarchy of their world, and it was definitely not on top. Eventually, Jethro found his place in the pack. As younger dogs would arrive on the mesa, I would see the same scenario play out again, with Jethro becoming one of those teaching them their place in dog world.

A few weeks after I bought Jethro home Jon rescued a one year old black and white parti poodle named Prince. Prince was the gentlest of dogs with the sweetest disposition. He was a bit awkward with the other dogs at first, as he did not seem accustomed to the sniffing rituals of being a dog. It took a bit of time but with Jon's loving patience Prince found his way in the pack. He and Jethro became the best of buddies.

With a new home, a new puppy, and a new job on the horizon, I waited for my family to visit for Thanksgiving. The airbnb I had rented back in August was two miles down the county road from where I was now living. When we had first made plans for them to visit, I was still living in T or C, never imagining I would be in Abiquiu when they actually arrived months later. Life kept layering one miracle upon another.

Another miracle appeared in a handful of stones. One early morning, I set out to hike with Jon and the dogs in our favorite arroyo. The arroyo was full of rugged canyon walls that were forever shifting their shapes. Pieces of soft sandstone lining the cliffs would fall away to create new craggy contours. High atop an outcropping, we discovered a mama owl sitting on a nest of twigs. We decided to be sure to return often to keep an eye out for babies. I picked up some stones that caught my eye that morning as we continued to hike. Collecting stones was not unusual in an area that abounds with fascinating specimens. Rocks and stones are everywhere, many of them multi-colored with glistening facets. What was unusual was the sense that these particular stones were speaking to me. As I carried them along the hike, ideas on teaching people how to build a personal mesa were being downloaded in my mind.

In the Andean tradition, a mesa is a shaman's portable altar, a handwoven textile containing stones, known as *kuyas*, that have been gathered from mountains or other places on Earth where one has a strong connection. I had been a mesa carrier since 2005 when I began training at the Four Winds Light Body School with Alberto Villoldo. The woven textile of a mesa is folded over in a square, with a beaded or woven band tied around the bundle to keep it secure. A mesa is opened during ceremony. To most people, it looks like a bag of stones or an arrangement of rocks. On a literal level, this is true, but at the mythic level, a mesa deepens your connection to Spirit and anchors you to Mother Earth. The only reason I had any sense of what the stones in the arroyo were speaking of was because of the connection to my own mesa.

I never had had any thought about teaching others to build a mesa, or even felt qualified to do so for that matter. Yet the ideas and inspiration I received on that early morning hike felt divinely inspired. I quickly began creating instructional videos. Our mesa-building course would be based on the cycles of the seasons, with each season becoming a mirror for our own self-reflection.

Our first season would be winter. The class opened in January with a despacho ceremony held in the arroyo where the stones had been found. Technology allowed the Mesa Building Journey to be offered online as well as on land. A large gathering of people from all over the world was able to participate. Our on-land gathering began with a small group ceremony. I returned to the arroyo in gratitude for the guidance on this first journey to build a personal mesa. We were embarking on a journey to deepen the connection to the ancient wisdom that lies in every rock and stone. Before heading into the arroyo, we prepared our luminous body with a white candle clearing to release energetic blocks by rolling the candle over our bodies. Then we carried the candles to our ceremonial site to burn.

It was a glorious day for ceremony in Abiquiu. After a chilly and overcast morning, the sun held us in warmth in the middle of winter. A beautiful herd of cattle met us at the entry point to our sacred site. As we are told in Animal Totems, a teaching of the StarStuffs spiritual website:

> *"Cows can teach us about home and community and the joy and contentment therein. Cows aid us in realizing to be easy going and live in the moment. They show us about love and connections at work and home. Cows can teach us how to make the changes needed to bring joy in our surroundings."*

It was a beautiful oracle for the journey we were about to embark on. As we began our trek through the arroyo, we found large stones to carry the burdens we were ready to release. This intention was shared with all those who had joined the journey online by blowing into the stones as we walked to our ceremonial site. We hiked a short distance through the canyon before turning off onto a rugged trail that opened into a clearing where the ground was flat, protected by the sandstone cliffs around us. It was there that we built an apuchetta, a small mountain of stones, with the rocks we had been carrying. Never had I felt like I was living my dharma, my deepest life purpose, more than at that time. Miracle upon miracle kept pouring into my life. Then I received a phone call—one that would intractably fracture the future of my family.

Releasing rituals are a powerful practice, especially when they are an ongoing part of your life. Tuning into the seasons or the cycles of the moon can be opportunities for such rituals. Before our despacho ceremony, we used white tapered candles for clearing. Without lighting the candle, roll it over your body while holding the intention of clearing the energetic patterns of fear or lack or any other negativity that has imprinted, shaped, and informed your being. Burn the candle outside somewhere away from your home to release these patterns. Clearing practices and releasing rituals begin to empty these energetic patterns of fear or lack and create a void in our field. In the presence of a void or vacuum, our energy field is going to look to fill up that space. Since an affinity for the patterns we are releasing is so strong, our field will naturally reshape itself to the previous pattern we just released. Thus, once we release something, we need to replace it at that same time with a new pattern. In this way, we are rebuilding our energy body, the luminous field that is informing and shaping our physical body.

How do we re-inform our luminous field after a clearing? What are you looking to create? If you are releasing lack, you may want to create abundance or prosperity. If you are releasing illness, then create optimum health. If you are releasing fear, then create love. There are endless qualities to be informed by other than fear. This is where affirmation and mantras will attune you to a new vibration, created through new thought patterns which can create new visions.

CHAPTER TWENTY-ONE

Wait

JETHRO AND I SETTLED INTO our life together on the mesa. I had been on the job making home visits through Presbyterian Española Hospital for about two months. These visits were an intimate way to come to know the community. The many generations of families that had called this place home welcomed me wholeheartedly each time I visited. I often left with homemade tortillas, fresh eggs from the chicken coop, or crisp apples from a fruit tree. My month-long mesa building class online had just been completed with the next session planned for spring.

I was getting ready for work on a mundane Monday morning when my phone rang. It was my daughter Danielle, barely audible through anguished sobs.

"Dad had a stroke," she cried.

It didn't seem possible. At fifty-six years old, Phil was one of the fittest people I knew. He was an endurance athlete who competed in triathlons, marathons, and even ultra-marathons where you run for a hundred miles. Through the numbing shock, I tried to reassure Danielle.

"If anyone can come through this, it's your dad," I told her. I truly believed it.

I had planned to be in New York that weekend to spend time with Phil and the family because his mother had died a few weeks earlier. I decided to wait until after the initial whirl of condolences had faded. My daughters were living with their dad full time for the first time since our divorce. The next day, my sister, Michele, called and said, "You need to get here as soon as possible. Phil is in a coma." Michele is a nurse. Her words were undeniable in their urgency. I arrived in New York two days later. Life had descended into an uncharted abyss that none of us knew how to navigate.

Phil was propped up slightly in a hospital bed in an ICU room. His eyes were closed. He had tubes in his nose and mouth. Next to the bed was a machine whose rhythmic drone was doing his breathing. Lines were attached to his ears and arms. Bags of fluids on metal poles dripped into his veins. Amid the beeps and alarms and mountains of medical intervention, I still believed Phil was going to make it.

It took doctors two days to figure out how someone as healthy as Phil could have suffered such massive bleeding to his brain. It turned out that for six weeks, he'd been running a low-grade fever. Because he was an endurance athlete a low grade fever was not enough to keep him laid up. A doctor had told him to take Tylenol. What was not known at the time was that Phil had picked up a staph infection at the hospital where he had spent untold hours with his dying mother. The infection was in his bloodstream. The bacteria and other blood components had formed a clot known as a vegetation on a heart valve. It eventually broke free and traveled to his brain. The bleeding it caused was so extensive that the neurologists said he would never recover beyond a vegetative state.

I still did not believe it was possible that Phil would not come through this. As a physical therapist, I have witnessed many miracles in my life: people walking after being told they would never walk again, living years after they were told they had six months left. I believed Phil had a miracle in him. For the sake of our daughters, he could not die.

Our vigil began. Sarabeth, Danielle, and I spent long hours in Phil's room. Nurses would step in and out to look at a machine or check his fluids, but most of the time, the room was occupied by the surge of friends, family, and colleagues shocked to see the man they knew as pulsing with vitality now relying on machines to stay alive. So many of the patients he had taught to walk with a prosthetic leg or had run marathons with were there too.

Danielle and Sarabeth were at his bedside through it all. I remember Sarabeth pleading, "Please don't leave me, Dad." More than I ever wanted anything in my life, I wanted Phil to live. Time seemed to stand still as he remained unresponsive. I felt he had to know we were there. He had to be able to feel the abundant and abiding love surrounding him. One of my Lodge Sisters told me that a few years earlier, she'd been in a coma for thirteen days: "They were ready to pull the plug. I could hear everything that was going on." She told me to keep stimulating his senses. "He is floating now," she said. I started rubbing his skin vigorously with a washcloth, praying he would return. For two weeks, we spent our days in the ICU holding his hand constantly, then sleeping at Phil's home at night.

Hours became days and days became weeks as I experienced an expansive sense of reality where nothing existed but love. There was no place for bitterness, anger, or resentment. Not knowing if Phil's next breath would be his last created a hyper-presence I had never known before. I remember wondering if this space of abiding love that I had been catapulted into could exist forever, as if I had been given an ephemeral brush with eternity.

After two weeks, Phil was moved to the hospice ward. The tubes, lines, alarms, and beeping machines were gone. The sparsely furnished room had a twin bed, a simple cushioned seat next to it, and a small nightstand with a lamp. We took turns sitting on that chair holding his hand. There was nothing else to do. I felt consumed with love.

Nearly forty-eight hours later, as Phil's hand rested in mine, an almost-imperceptible shift occurred, as if something had very gently slipped away. I wasn't sure if he had died. I couldn't tell if he was breathing. "Is he gone?" I thought. I never expected to be so intimate with my former husband's passing. As I held his hand in those final weeks, I remember saying to Phil, "I must be the last person you ever imagined would be here."

I went to get a nurse who confirmed that Phil had died. My daughters were inconsolable. They had watched their dad slip away with a strength beyond their young years. Now, the finality of death had irrevocably changed their lives. "He looks so old," Danielle said. It was true. I had never been with someone at the moment they died. Once the life force left his body, it looked as if Phil aged ten years in just a few moments.

My daughters were suffering in ways I could never even begin to imagine. The house they lived in with him was now empty of their father.

I'd been away from my new job and Jethro longer than I ever imagined. Jon was a lifeline as he lovingly took on the tasks of caring for Jethro, but the lifeline to my job felt tenuous. I had just started a few months ago. Now I was needing extended time away. I could not bear leaving my daughters but found it hard to be gone from my job without losing it altogether. I was feeling a kinship with the mama owl Jon and I had discovered in the high cliffs of the arroyo as she patiently sits and waits for her babies to leave the nest. Sarabeth and Danielle were far from babies, but as humans, we need so much more time. I struggled about leaving them and worried if they were ready. Phil's death felt as if they were prematurely being pushed out of the nest whether they were ready or not.

Phil's orthodox sister planned his burial. I planned a secular memorial service. Over a thousand people showed up. I have no idea how all of these plans came together in such a short time. The void left once Phil was gone from our lives would take many years of stumbling before it felt as if some ground was beneath our feet again. After a year and a half without the mortgage being paid, Phil's house went into foreclosure. Sarabeth found an apartment, and Danielle moved in with her boyfriend, Mike. Six years later, she gave birth to my first granddaughter. They named her Philippa.

On the day of Phil's stroke, colleagues told me, someone had called him in his office and heard only a garbled sound on the phone. They thought it was a joke and went to Phil's office to see what he was up to. He was slumped in a chair, unable to move, repeatedly uttering the word *wait.*

Wait.

That was it.

Wait.

I know that in those moments before he would lose all consciousness, Phil knew what was happening was serious. He may have even had a sense that death was near. In that moment, he was bargaining with death.

"But wait I haven't ..."

"But wait I didn't ..."

"But wait I need to ..."

The scene haunts me to this day.

Phil had reason to fear death: other men in his family had died young. Even for those without specific cause, death remains our greatest fear, something we stuff in the dark crypts of our hearts. The only thing we know for certain is that death will come. What does that mean for this fleeting life we are given? How do we spend our time in our very brief stay on Earth? We have been given a body to create this life here. How do we know if we have done that well? How do we live so that our one fleeting life matters to the world? Imagine if death were to come what regrets might you have about your life.

As I sat writing this manuscript over the years, a thought gnawed at me when I wanted to give up. My greatest regret would be not finishing this book before I died. I wanted to fulfill that prophecy foretold by a shaman in Peru. What would you regret not creating with your life before you die? Can you take a step in the direction of your dreams today?

CHAPTER TWENTY-TWO

The Runaway Puppy

IT WAS HEARTBREAKING TO RETURN home with my daughters' lives upended. Danielle begged me not to go. I knew I could not rely on Jon to take care of Jethro forever. Plus I had a job I needed to hold on to. I vowed to return to New York as often as I could to help my daughters, even if only for long weekends.

Although my job was still there when I returned to New Mexico six weeks after leaving it, I was also made aware of how difficult it had been on the homecare team while I was away. I traveled back to New York many times over that year. Even though we had been divorced for fifteen years, Phil's death still ripped through my life like the aftershocks of an earthquake. What was most troubling was the uncertainty as to where Sarabeth and Danielle would live. I felt as if I needed to be both in New Mexico for my job and in New York for my daughters. I remember the advice I received from the same friend who thought I should adopt Jethro. "If you go back to save your daughters," she told me, "they will never know they can get through this on their own. You can help them but you don't need to rescue them."

When I arrived back in New Mexico, I headed to Jon's to pick up Jethro. He had grown so much since I'd last seen him only six weeks earlier. His floppy ears had begun to perk up as he continued growing out of puppyhood. He was so excited to see me. I was afraid he might have forgotten me altogether while I was gone. Before I left Jon told me, "I need to take a break from our relationship. I started dating someone and want to get the relationship on solid ground before you and I see each other again."

He figured he needed about a month. I was shocked. I had no idea he was interested in seeing anyone else. The fragments of my fragile heart felt as if they were losing their tenuous hold on life. I fell in love with Jon when he dropped the rose petals on my back. I had never stopped loving him. I left his home numb, unable to feel a thing.

The next day, Jethro ran away. We had taken a walk along the dirt road around our small community. It was early evening when a crack of thunder rumbled over the mesa. It must have been the first time Jethro ever heard the sound, and he ran off into the wilderness. I followed him for as long as I could but soon lost sight of him. I walked and ran through the hills and arroyos for hours calling his name. The sky turned dark as night fell. I returned home alone.

I was broken. Losing Jethro seemed to rip away what little hold on life was left. I couldn't bear one more loss. I wanted the world to stop spinning and let me off. I was isolated in a remote terrain which I now called home. I cried myself to sleep believing Jethro was gone forever. I cried for my daughters who had lost their dad on the threshold of young adulthood. I cried for the tragic death of a man whose life had been woven into the fabric of my family for thirty years. I cried for my own shattered dreams ravaged in illusions. I cried for the wasted years playing a fool in love. I cried for my failures as a wife, a mother, a lover, a friend. I cried for all the people I had let down, the mistakes I had made. I cried for relief from unbearable pain.

Although Jon wanted a month-long break, I let him know about Jethro's disappearance. He immediately began printing three-foot color photographs of Jethro that we pasted onto neon poster boards on stakes along highways and county roads. We put up flyers at the post office and the local market, Bode's. We spent hours after I returned from work walking the mesa calling out his name.

After three nights away, Jethro came home. He showed up at the front door while I was at work. My landlord called to let me know she'd let him in. I couldn't believe my eyes when I returned home that day. I looked straight at a miracle when I walked through the door. Jethro looked a little worn. His appetite was huge and he slept a bit more than usual, but his spunk returned the next day.

Unexpectedly, the loss of Jethro had brought Jon back into my life because of our mutual love for Jethro and all his help trying to find him. The month-long break never happened. The new romance he had started was short-lived. Jethro's return was a spark of light through the pervasive darkness that had descended through so much loss. I can't tell you where the idea came from, but the thought of writing a children's story about Jethro's runaway penetrated the barren emptiness of my psyche. Never in my life had I ever thought to write a children's story. A story like that would mean I'd have to make up what happened to Jethro during those three nights he was gone. I was much more comfortable writing non-fiction.

Sensibly, I dismissed the idea entirely, but that did not make it go away. Little scenes and conversations kept showing up in my head. I was finding inspiration for characters from the wildlife on the mesa. My first attempts were lame, but writing Jethro's story became a lifeline to the other side of the grief that had enveloped me since Phil's death.

Once I started on that path, one of my first stops was the principal's office at Abiquiu Elementary School. I needed help making up stories about Jethro's wilderness adventure, since I had no idea what happened to him while he was gone. I thought, "What better way to write a children's story than through the unencumbered imagination of children?" I told the school's principal, Claudia Sena, about my idea of collaborating with the pupils there to help finish the story. She had no idea how her wholehearted acceptance of the project became a beacon helping me navigate my life through a time of painful darkness.

Meeting the students was an opportunity to listen to their stories. Most of the children in rural northern New Mexico have dogs in their lives. Many had stories of their own dogs' running away. Not all of them ended with the dog's return. They shared openly and innocently their stories of death and loss, joy and laughter. Jethro's story lived in their own. In writing Jethro's tale, I wanted them to see their own precious stories, ones that weave themselves into the tapestry of love lost and love returned through the uncontainable cycles of life. Jethro's story was a mystery beyond my comprehension. Perhaps the mystery is simply not ours to comprehend, just something to be lived, for miracles can lie in loss, in heartache, in loneliness and despair.

We are human, with the flaws and limitations, heartache and pain, that come with this privilege. We are also divine, birthed from a love that pulses as light. In this lovelight is the power to create human life, the same source that births our dreams and visions through the sacred alchemy of light.

Pouring myself into this project with the students of Abiquiu Elementary was an unexpected source of enlightenment through one of the darkest storms of my life. Death upends everything. I was staring into an abyss with no guideposts on what life would look like for me or my daughters without Phil in it. Pouring myself into writing Jethro's story was a divine mystery, a source of inspiration guided by the innocence of children. The source of the idea could only be called a divine blessing. Spirit heard the cries of my heart. Although I tried to push away the thought of writing a children's story, it persisted. I am so grateful that I listened, for Jethro's story became a guiding light through the darkness. Spirit may not call in expected ways, but when we hear it and heed it, our life can find miracles through the bleakest of times. Do not discount your intuition or what others may consider crazy.

CHAPTER TWENTY-THREE

Betrayal

AFTER LIVING IN MY CASITA for two years, the landlord put it up for sale, along with the main house next to it and the ten acres of land they sat on. It was more property and more money than I could manage. Finding another rental in the remote rural community was challenging. The area was becoming increasingly popular in the airbnb market leaving long term renters like me in a state of drought. The two story stone and adobe artist studio that stood across from the casita I was renting unexpectedly became available. The owner had a deal fall through. I wondered if I should approach him about buying his place? There were two things I had told myself since moving to New Mexico that I did not want. One was a mortgage; the other was a home that relied on burning wood to stay warm. I got both.

The fascinating house that I had photographed years earlier on the Abiquiu Studio Tour was now mine. Never was there a glimpse that I would someday own that home when I first stepped into it. I had never even believed I could buy a house on my own. My eight-year-old self would be incredibly proud of me. Mortgage rates were historically low, making my monthly payment just a little more than the $600 I had been paying in rent. My daughter, Danielle, loaned me $10,000 for a down payment, which I repaid in a few years. Unknown to any of us, Phil had generous life insurance policies for both my daughters. The money was an unexpected source of stability through the upheaval left by his death.

The daily rhythm of living on the mesa barely changed, but now—for the first time ever—I was living in a home that was all mine. As with most things since I'd relocated to New Mexico, the move was effortless. Jon and a couple of our friends carried my possessions across the half-acre between my new home and my old one, the first time I ever moved without a truck or trailer from U-Haul.

In addition to the five acres, I now also owned the scattered piles of weathered window frames, old doors, abandoned timber boxes, and all kinds of other wood just lying around the property that the artist before me had left. Eventually, these piles of trash transformed themselves into a glass-topped dining table, a storage shed for tools and wood, a fence marking the property line, an outdoor pergola, and side tables in and around the house.

The rustic recycling reminded me of the arts-and-crafts projects from my childhood when I used to visit my Aunt Eileen for a week every summer at my grandparents' white clapboard bungalow in Mastic Beach on Long Island. There was no heat, no phone, an outhouse, and an outdoor well, but there was always plenty to keep me busy. I made fruit bowls out of popsicle sticks, wove pot holders on tiny looms, and poured melted wax over ice cubes in milk cartons to make candles. Transforming the piles of trash that came with the land into treasures for my home felt as if Aunt Eileen's arts-and-crafts projects had come of age.

Over the years, daily life on the mesa had shaped itself around Jon and the posse of dogs we called family—a family born out of big sky, dusty soil, high desert terrain, and above all else love; love for the land, love for the dogs and what I thought was love for each other. Although we had been the sexiest of lovers, my relationship with Jon at this stage of life rarely involved sex. When I first moved to Abiquiu, I'd imposed an unspoken rule on myself: I would not initiate sex with him. The endless breakups we'd suffered through made it feel too vulnerable. Waiting for Jon to initiate love-making often took years, but no matter how long I waited, I always responded with an amorous yes.

Instead of being lovers, we became affectionate friends, best friends. Jon was my nearest and dearest. Foot massages, back rubs, Thai massage, and hugs formed an intimate physical framework for our relationship. Whenever we crossed the line into love-making, it was achingly familiar in the best way possible. Still, the deepest aspects of the relationship between us remained unspoken. All of our decisions about whether to have sex or not were happening without any conversation about the state of our relationship or who we were in each other's lives. We never talked about where our relationship was going but to me the relationship felt like it was where it would always be. I could never imagine my life in Abiquiu without Jon. He felt as ever-present to me as the flat-topped Pedernal on the horizon.

Without ongoing sex, our relationship deepened in many other ways. Jon and I spent our time walking Jethro and Prince around the mesa along with a vagabond posse of neighborhood dogs. We often ventured with our dogs to meadows and forest trails on the way to Chama, where we even spent a winter season snowshoeing. We took weekend getaways farther north to Eagle Nest and Red River. We traveled to neighboring Colorado to explore Boulder, Salida, and Durango. On weekly errands to Santa Fe, we splurged on raw turkey necks for the dogs at the high-end pet food store Marty's Meals that they devoured with abandon. We left hot yoga classes dripping in sweat and chanted Wahe Guru in Kundalini classes at Yogi Bhajan's ashram in Española. It was a simple life, with Jon and the dogs at the very heart of it all.

Although we sometimes treated ourselves to expensive dinners in Santa Fe, meals at Jon's house were absolutely my favorite. His skills far surpassed my own, and he could turn the most mundane chicken thigh into a culinary masterpiece with exotic spices, caramelized Brussels sprouts, or roasted lemon rinds. I was happy to be his sous chef following directions on chopping or peeling. Jon was the most sensual man I had known. He savored food with every sense in his body. Dinner with him was a submergence in pleasure. It was also what made him such an exquisite lover. Although I had learned to brace myself during sex, Jon is forever the one to strip me free of the armor in my body and feel its orgasmic pleasure.

The only time we talked about our relationship was when Jon was planning a vacation with a friend from New York. She was the other situation he had in mind when I first tried to kiss him during our Contact Yoga practice decades earlier. In the twenty years I had known Jon, I had never seen them together and never understood the nature of their relationship. Was it a friendship? Were they getaway lovers? My only view of the relationship was through whatever lens or filter Jon chose. It was easy to believe she didn't exist—until they went on vacation together.

Once or twice a year, she planned extravagant excursions for them to luxury lodges in national parks, Art Deco tours in Palm Springs, Broadway shows, and exclusive art openings in New York. The only time her name would come up was when he was going away and plans needed to be made for me to watch Prince. I tried to understand who she was to him. Calling up every ounce of courage, I'd ask some awkward question like, "Are you going to have sex with her?" "There's always a possibility," he said. Sex seemed like the barometer to me of how close they were. In my mind, his answer meant maybe yes, maybe no. I liked to think it was no. Even though Jon and I were not lovers, having sex with her would put her on some higher relationship status than with me, which kept my mind jumping through convoluted loops to try and make sense of this other situation.

Without any information, I was left filling in gaps and making up stories in my head. Jon would return after a week away relieved to be home. He was more of a homebody than a traveler, and I wondered how much he enjoyed going places. It often seemed as if his time away had been a chore, and I kept hoping—and truly believing—that one day, he would tire of the situation. By default I would then be elevated to the one and only in his life as the last woman standing.

While he was away, there were no calls or texts. It felt as if I didn't exist. It stirred up every belief I'd ever had that I was not enough. After a week, he would return, and it could be another year before he saw her again.

I endured the inflexible parameters of our relationship through my own vanity, naivete, and, perhaps more important, the wall of secrecy that Jon maintained around this other relationship. I was able to see him and touch him and be with him every day, yet a covert competition was endlessly playing out. It filled me with fear that if I did something to upset him or drive him away, he always had someone else to go to. He had a backup plan. He would never truly have to be alone.

Our relationship existed in a tight box which I stayed inside of because I feared that if I stepped outside, I would lose him. The consequences would be too great if I expressed anger or frustration or said how I truly felt. Any uncomfortable conversations we had about feelings would ultimately culminate in silence between us. Silence was a sword that was used to inflict pain by completely withdrawing love and attention from each other. The emotional freeze would take a few days to thaw and we would re-enter each other's lives again, never to speak of what had created the chasm in the first place. These patterns were longstanding between us, and had played a large part in my decision to protect myself around sex when I first arrived there.

Despite the emotional dysfunction, I loved spending time with Jon. He was my dearest friend. He made me laugh more than anyone with his endearing sense of humor. There was a comfort and ease that came from the history that had carried us through decades together. Yet the shadow that wrapped this deep familiarity was also what fed my fears and insecurities. I was afraid to ask for what I really wanted and what I really wanted was him. My deepest desire was for us to fully embrace each other in a relationship, for him to want me as much as I wanted him. The disappointment if I asked for this and didn't get it felt too great to bear. Instead, I clung tenaciously to the dream that someday, I would have Jon all to myself.

Once Covid hit, travel stopped for both of us. With social distancing the new normal, we were the only ones in each other's bubble. It drew us even closer. I thought perhaps his relationship in New York had faded, since years went by without his seeing her. As the doors to the world started to open again I had a visit planned to New York to visit my daughters.

After taking the dogs for a walk along the dirt road that encircled the mesa, we sat on the tailgate of Jon's 4-Runner. My visit to New York was coming up in a week. Jon was checking to confirm dates since Jethro would be with him while I was gone. That was our usual arrangement. He was planning to be in New York to attend a birthday party for his ninety-year-old aunt right after I got back. I was reluctant to ask about his plans figuring they might involve seeing his friend. It always took a lot of internal fortitude for me to ask about matters involving his New York friend. I mustered the courage, sounding as casual as I could and asked, "What is happening with your trip to New York?"

The birthday party for his aunt had turned into a month-long road trip with his New York friend. He was picking her up in Albuquerque the day after I got home so they could drive to New York together as a test drive for getting married.

I was engulfed by an earthquake, my life crumbling beneath my feet. To say I was blindsided was an understatement. Our lives were intertwined with each other every day. We were mom and pop to our dogs. While we took them on walks, ate dinners together, ran errands to Santa Fe, watched our favorite TV shows, gave and received back rubs and foot massages lying together on his couch—while our lives were happening together, he was coming up with this plan to get married. His relationship with her was no secret, yet I never imagined his feeling running so deep that he wanted to marry her. Any dreams I had of ever being with him were being shattered.

Once I returned from New York, he and Prince were gone. The day-to-day rituals that created the intimate framework of my life disappeared overnight. Communication between us was severed immediately. I lost my best friend, and so did Jethro. Abiquiu suddenly felt like the loneliest place in the world.

I think I teeter-totter in a way that must be hard to see which way I am leaning from day to day. In a way that you really don't know if you have my support, my embrace. If I am just biding my time here.

The words he had written decades earlier seemed more relevant than ever. The answer was finally clear. All these years, I had been nothing more than a convenient companion, an affectionate friendship, as he had, in fact, just been biding his time. There had always been some kind of divine thread that held us together despite our estrangements. This time the chasm felt too wide to recover from, the damage too deep to repair. Since he was committed to moving his life in this other direction there was no need for me to be a part of it anymore. I got back from my visit to New York and he was gone.

How could I not see this coming? In my wildest dreams I never could have imagined the miracles that opened doors and ushered me to a life where in the entire state of New Mexico I had landed less than three miles from Jon. The well of miracles that seemed to confirm the destiny of our being together had finally run dry, leaving me forsaken on dark and lonely shores.

Letting go of Jon meant letting go of my innermost fears of being alone and abandoned. It meant letting go of the attachment to a corrupted version of love that I had believed to be true. Staying bound to a belief I would never be loved had kept me in a relationship where no matter what I did or who I was, I would never be enough. Jon had chosen another woman over me, confirming those beliefs I held about myself.

To feel all these things was bitterly painful. But it was also the only way I would ever free myself from the limits and constrictions I had trapped myself in. I had poured all of my love into Jon, hoping it would be returned so he would love all the places in me that I deemed unlovable. What was left when our relationship ended was an absence of love, not for him but for me. There was no special moment of grace, no magical guru appeared. It was only me, face to face with all the ways I had abandoned my own heart.

My seeking for something outside myself to satisfy my ravenous craving for love had always been doomed.

The response I was trying to get from Jon was the same manipulative love dance I had done with my father as a child. I simply wanted my dad to love me, without needing to feel like I had to shape myself into something I thought he wanted in order to get that love. Nothing else and no one else could satisfy the unquenchable thirst, for the cup was mine to fill. I was the one I had been searching for. I so desperately wanted to write a happily-ever-after story, like the childhood fables full of princesses preaching that the way to feminine attainment was to marry the prince. The fairy tales were only a corrupted version of feminine fulfillment much like the false prophets of beauty that had appeared within me on the holy mountain Umantay.

What I clearly saw once Jon was gone was that the love I was seeking was my own. I had wanted him to change my underserving self into someone who was worthy of love. I was the one who needed my love. Jon was the crutch I had used to prop up my broken self. Once the crutch was gone, I was left face to face with my own debilitating woundedness. That spring, historic wildfires ravaged northern New Mexico. Ominous plumes of smoke sat on the horizon for months, looking like the aftermath of an atomic bomb. Their unwavering presence was a constant reminder of death and destruction. It was as if the only way the cords that tethered my life to Jon could be severed were through my own apocalyptic fire that was incinerating the life I was living.

Sitting on a shelf in my home like an ornate decoration was a sixteen-inch frame drum made by a local drum maker. After Jon was gone, I picked it up. I took the wooden stick with the red suede fringe at its handle and the stuffed buckskin on top and began beating. The drumbeat aroused a voiceless voice that gave rise to longings not heard and desires unmet. The drumbeat awoke a heart numbed by oppression through insufferable heartaches. It reached back to the wounds of ancestors and called out to unnamed spirits for relief.

The drumbeat was a song whose rhythms rode on the humiliation of having played a fool in love for so long. The beat was the heartbeat of the unending love of our Earth Mother, her womb an archive of the suffering since time immemorial. So many voices had inhabited my inner landscape telling me who I was. These voices of lack had become my identity. The voice now singing carried discordant tunes and desolate tears in search of peace.

How many times have we been punished simply for having a voice? Or being too loud? Or making too much noise? Our voice, our sound is our unique expression. Find it and let it be a prayer. All these voices that play in our head have a frequency. They inform us with their vibrations, and when the voices create thoughts that are oppressive, they weigh heavy on our soul. We can create new frequencies and vibrations, with sound and thought, prayer and song. How do we find this soul song? Breathe into the earth as you sit upon her. Feel your breath in and out through your pelvis. When you are ready, when it feels natural, make a sound on the exhale—any sound, a tone, it doesn't matter. Continue like this, breathing in and then sounding on your exhale. Allow your voice to be free. Give yourself freedom and permission to make a sound, to make noise, to be heard.

Many of us were told to be quiet. Our voice had to shape itself in order to be loved. Maybe you grew up with the creed that children were to be seen but not heard. Maybe your sound is a hum, maybe a vowel sound, maybe the sounds link together in a short harmony or rhythm. As you sing these sounds, they are your soul song. As you sing, offer this soul song to the Earth, to God/Goddess, to Spirit.

You can sing your soul song into a stone and place it on the earth to let your vibration weave itself into all of nature. Imagine a stone resting on the Earth with the soul song from each one of us reverberating into the world. You can sing your soul song to your garden or into seeds before you plant them and allow your song to blossom and bear fruit. Listen to the sounds around you. It is as if all of nature is always in prayer, always in song. This is your nature too. Our original face, our original song is a discovery waiting within. It begins with a sound.

CHAPTER TWENTY-FOUR

The Way of Darkness

OVER THE YEARS, I CULTIVATED the land around my home. I planted western cottonwoods and aspen trees. I transplanted golden chamisa and purple Russian sage. There were ornamental grasses and yellow daffodil bulbs. I created gravel walkways and rock gardens. I built outdoor planters out of scraps of adobe brick adorned with spikes of yucca. The land around my house was a blank canvas when I arrived. My garden unearthed an inner artist that filled me with delight through every season. As happens every spring, extensive clearing of the land was needed after a winter of hibernation.

Jon left in early April. Once he was gone, every fiber of my being was poured into the garden. I made a small prayer bundle into which I blew all the sorrow and ache that arose from this belief of not-enough. As I burned the weeds I pulled, I let the prayer bundle burn with it. It felt reminiscent of the cleaning and clearing of the ceremony to sell my home over a decade ago.

It was so hard to extricate Jon from my life in New Mexico. He was woven into my soul as much as the mountains surrounding me and the big sky air I breathed. I had suffered many losses in my life but none had come with the searing sword of betrayal. We had no conversation about what had changed his affection or led to his departure.

I told no one. When neighbors and friends asked where Jon was, I would nonchalantly say he was tending to family matters in New York. My daughter, Danielle, visited about a month after he left, bringing her husband, Mike, and my granddaughter, Philippa, for the first time. Under normal circumstances, we would have spent time with Jon. Instead I told them he was in New York but didn't say why. The lies engulfed me in shame. They hid things not only from the outside world but from myself as well. There was shame in presenting a relationship to the world that was nothing more than a prop. It reached back to a childhood lived in chaos behind closed doors. Shame hid in a marriage that could never fulfill its picture perfect dream, and shame was cloaked in the secret failures of a woman afraid to speak the truth.

Once Jon left, I was catapulted into an unexpected retreat that reminded me of being lost on the mountain. Although the elements of my surrounding did not impose the danger the high desert wilderness had, the embattled terrain of my heart felt just as precarious. When I thought about Jon's forsaking me to marry someone else, I couldn't imagine what my life in New Mexico would look like without him in it. He was the reason I was here. His decision to leave made me question every choice that had come before. Was there even a purpose to my being here? Had I done the right thing by creating so much distance from my family? Was moving to New Mexico the most colossal mistake I ever made in my life?

Nature was my restoration. Hands in soil, feet in dirt became a curative medicine much like walking barefoot on the Earth after Jon's mother died. I returned to our favorite arroyo, where we had spent endless hours hiking with Jethro and Prince. I had held ceremony in that arroyo for the mesa building class I created when I first arrived. I had prayed into a myriad of untold stones along its path. The arroyo had taken me, Jon and the dogs into the high desert wilderness free of cars, concrete, and people. We walked uncharted paths often feeling as if we were on land no one else had traveled. In Peru, they call the mountains undomesticated. Land that is undomesticated has a palpable wildness. The arroyo was wild, infused with our thousands of steps and countless breaths intermixed with the untold memories of walking through these canyon walls.

On my first visit to New Mexico, I had hiked this arroyo with Jon. After about an hour, we came to a large gray boulder about four feet around bulging out of the earth. Nature had sculpted it to look like a massive head. Dark markings etched along its side seemed like eyes. A slightly curved slit in front gave the impression of a mouth. Together, it looked like a mammoth turtle head breaking its way out of a mound of dirt. It became a marker for how far we had hiked. Each time we made it to the turtle, we felt as if we were encountering an old friend.

In the winter after Jon left, I returned to walk the arroyo with Jethro. I was acutely aware of the changes since I'd first set foot there thirteen years earlier. Boulders and stones had fallen from canyon walls that could no longer be contained by the sandstone cliffs holding them. Paths had been altered and the landscape transformed by the waters, winds, snow, and ice. As nature had reshaped its contours over the years, it was reflecting the essence of our human life. Our walls collapse. Our worlds shift and collide. The raging waters all around feel as if they will sweep us away.

As I walked through this familiar yet transforming landscape, I was struck by its incredible beauty, a holy beauty that had eluded me on the mountain Umantay in Peru. Everything was astounding in beauty, from the dusting of snow that spattered the highest cliffs to the crumbling walls where dripping snow soaked into the red soil. The stillness steeped the arroyo in an immense silence. Not a silence that inflicts pain but a mother tongue with a meaning beyond mere words. I felt the great privilege of being human and the boundless gift we have been given in our planet Earth.

I carried items for a ceremony. I wanted to leave an offering at the turtle, a site I held sacred in my relationship with Jon. I found a bird feeder made of seeds in the shape of a heart at Bode's, our local general store. It fit in the palm of my hand. It became my k'intu, my prayer holder in lieu of coca or bay leaves. In a small pouch, I carried feathers, dried corn, and flowers. As I hiked the arroyo held in the infinite wisdom of our Earth Mother, I blew the sorrows of my heart into my prayer holder. I blew in the tears over the loss of Jon and Prince from my life. I blew in deep gratitude for every step I had taken and for the benevolent beauty in which I was held. I walked the arroyo as if I was kissing the Earth with my feet. As I saw the turtle off in the distance, my heart opened in kinship. There are few other places on Earth where my connection feels so deep. I laid the birdseed heart on the turtle's crown and adorned her with the feathers, flowers, and dried corn. I imagined the birds and animals of the arroyo coming to take the seeds and carry them great distances in the same way the wishes of a child are scattered on the seeds of a dandelion.

Sometime after this simple ceremony, I came across these words written by Jess Hagan about turtle medicine:

> *Enduring a low-grade unhappiness will only perpetuate more of that unhappiness. Learning to enjoy the way wanting feels brings what we want to us with swift and easy grace because it is the sensation of the thing we are after, not the thing itself.*

Enduring a low-grade unhappiness resonated with me deeply. That was the state of my being long before Jon. What was most profound to read was, "Learning to enjoy the way wanting feels brings what we want to us with swift and easy grace." The way wanting felt terrified me. In a story my family retold throughout my childhood, I always had a bottle hanging from my mouth, whether there was milk in it or not, until I was about three years old. It must have offered comfort, much like a glorified pacifier. My family tried hard to rid me of this bottle.

"You're a big girl. Big girls don't have bottles."

"Look at how silly you look with that bottle hanging out of your mouth."

"Give me that bottle or you're going to get a spanking."

When threats and shame didn't work, they turned to my grandfather to break the habit. As the story goes, my bottle was taken away one summer night and I was left alone at the bungalow with my grandfather, who was hard of hearing and the only one who could tolerate my screams. With no consolation, I eventually passed out, most likely from an overdose of devastation and exhaustion. The supposed moral of the story was that I was cured. I never asked for the bottle again.

Much later in life, though, I came to see that the real moral of the story was that I was left afraid to want anything. The more we want something, the deeper the pain when it is gone. At three years old, the loss of my bottle was intolerable. It is too simplistic to say that the bottle trauma was at the root of all the ills in my life but it did leave an imprint. Not only was the bottle torn away but so too were the feelings of pleasure and comfort that came with it. Learning to enjoy the way wanting felt left me scared to death, the same fear Dr. Lowen had seen when he looked deep in my eyes years ago. The abrupt and devastating rupture of Jon's presence in my life seemed to have energetic cords, as the shamans call them, that reached back to that moment when my bottle was ripped from my world.

It would be nearly a year before I could say the words "Jon is getting married" to any family or friends. Some people in our community told me that when they heard the news, they thought he was marrying me. To the community, we appeared to be together. A memory came back of a pendant Jon had given me early in our relationship.

It was sterling silver about the size of a quarter hanging on a thin silver chain. The Om symbol was engraved in its center, surrounded by a seven-petal lotus flower with the symbol for each chakra embossed in each petal. I wore it constantly. On my first trip to Peru, after Jon had left for New Mexico, I took off the pendant and left it on the sacred stones at Machu Picchu. The offering was both a good-bye and a wish to see him again.

It was there, with the shamans at Machu Picchu, that marked the start of my journey to the Divine Feminine. Their ceremonies and initiations felt beyond my understanding while I traveled with them. My Western mindset was coming face-to-face with a cosmology built around right relationship with all of Nature, one with reverence for the Earth and the mountains, the sky and the stars. As we traveled through Peru together, the shamans spoke of women as visionaries, with the potential to be midwives of change by walking in balance between the Masculine and Feminine. Inside of me, I heard their words as truth. My journey had begun.

Still heartbroken nearly a year after Jon left, I took a shamanic journey. These have always been a way for me to seek clarity or understanding from dimensions beyond my small mind and limited beliefs. In my home, while lying on my back with eyes covered, the sound of rhythmic drumming guided me to a state of conscious dreaming. As often happened, I found myself at a cave or some sort of portal at the start of a journey.

Walking through the dark cave, I came across petroglyphs etched into the walls, and ran my hands over them as I went on. Around a bend, I could see daylight ahead. I followed the light to a large grassy meadow full of wildflowers. Mountains were all around. Two horses stood in the field. Jon was on one of them. I sat in the saddle on the other. Both Jon and I were wearing cowboy hats as we meandered through the field on our horses. We had never ridden horses together in real life. One thing that stood out on this shamanic journey was that there was no rush, no sense of needing to get anywhere or be someplace. It seemed to reflect the nature of my relationship with Jon: both lovely and aimless. We came to a stream. The horses stopped to drink. As I looked into the water, I was captivated by how it glistened, sparkling like crystals. In the next moment, I found myself swept into the current, which went rushing over a waterfall. I heard the words, "This is the part of the journey that you must take by yourself."

Tumbling down the waterfall felt as if I was suspended in time. I was falling through space, not in a tumultuous way but floating free, riding an endless waterfall. Finally, the fall stopped. I landed in nothingness, in complete and utter darkness. Nothing to see, nothing I could hold on to. All I felt was fear—of the dark, of not knowing where I was, of the unknown and my inability to see a single thing. My sense of being kept sinking deeper and deeper into this void, and eventually I could feel myself being held in it. The caress of the darkness was softening my fear. Dropping deeper into the darkness was like being held in the womb. Words came through once again: "There is a way for you to see in this darkness. It is your intuition. It is your inner knowing. You know your way here."

This was a knowing not based on the mind nor facts nor any scientific data to prove its worth. It was a deep knowing that knows what is truth, the deepest power of the Divine Feminine. It was a journey to the seedling of that sacred power, a journey that had started twenty years earlier on a holy mountain in Peru. As with any sacred journey, what seems like a walk through fire is required for our limited beliefs to burn up and die. I kept holding on to the belief of a happily-ever-after relationship with Jon. In that story, I would feel complete as a woman. My cup would be full. Happiness would reign for the rest of my days. This was the fabricated path to the most powerful manifestation of the Divine Feminine that lived in my head. It was not where truth would be found.

I never fully understood my relationship with Jon. Never had I made the sacrifices to be with someone that I did for him. The crumbs I settled for were such a poor investment of my heart. It made no sense for me to be so deeply attached for so very long to a relationship where my voice was not heard and my love was unrequited. Yet our relationship often seemed divinely orchestrated beyond anything I could have created through my own mortal will. Everything from the snow blessing that brought us back together before Jon left New York to the wave of miracles that ushered me to my life in Abiquiu seemed mystical.

My shamanic journey had pushed me higher on the mountain to where I could see how the path I had stepped onto twenty years earlier to awaken the Divine Feminine could not have happened without Jon. He had whirled into my life on a spinning dance invoking Aphrodite, initiated by an offering left on sacred stones at Machu Pichu. Our journey was a quest for me to discover the source of the Divine Feminine, something that could only be unearthed by a scorching shamanic fire—the death of our relationship.

My day-to-day life with Jon shrouded this awareness of the force of my Divine Feminine power. The shamanic journey was a penetrating truth that obliterated the way I had seen our relationship. What I could sense was an abiding love not attached to objects or circumstances. This burgeoning awareness was a recognition of who we are simply as love, a love that is not washed away when the tides of life bring great loss.

Death is unavoidable. The shamans of Peru speak of it as a beloved. They do not fear death. The shamans we traveled with deeply trust the wisdom of Nature. They respect unwaveringly the cycles of death and rebirth that emerge again and again. They know that death is a portal. I came to see that Jon was my portal to the Divine Feminine. My journey with him was an initiation into the dark mysteries of her power. My endless seeking had exhausted itself in the name of love. I never imagined that the nightmare of Jon's marrying another woman would be a path to enlightenment.

When it came, enlightenment did not arrive tied up neatly in a tidy box with an immaculate bow. It came to me through a path that was fraught with struggle and conflict, devastating loss, and the sword of betrayal. Even the nightmare of Jon's marrying another woman was a gift. It was a gift that would take nearly two years for me to open in order to see the blessing that lay in a battered box of pain and loss. I was holding on to an outdated belief that it was unbefitting for a woman to be without a man, that a woman on her own was lacking in some way. It was the way I'd begun dimming my light in the first place, to get a boy to like me. I was doing the same thing with Jon by keeping myself small, never making demands on his time lest I push him away.

Seeing this, I could see how I was linked to the way women who had come before me had moved through darkness to a place of light. I thought about my mother, who had risen through hardship to the throne she sits on as our family's shining matriarch. Since my father died, she has lived on her own, her survival no longer dependent on a man. She is a beacon of light to all who know her. Though our family is scattered among many states, she has found a way to keep us connected. Despite coming to technology late in life, she started a family group text many years ago. Each morning, she sends uplifting messages and photos from the Daily Word, which she reads every day.

My mother remembers every birthday, anniversary, and date of every family member who has died. Each date is remembered on our group texts with a flurry of photos. An entire wall in her home is dedicated to pictures of our family that she has framed over the years. My mother is the keeper of our family history. She has calendars that date back decades, and friends she has known since kindergarten. There is no one else in our family who holds this treasure trove.

My Aunt Eileen is one of the most beloved women in our family. She never married, never had children. She always lived alone. She sustained herself by creating a life of friendships, a life where she was able to support herself financially and eventually own her own home. Our phone conversations wrap me in her humor and her unwavering love for me.

The words that Don Andreas spoke to me in that coca leaf reading years before assured me that the Apus would help me. Though I could not see how a Spirit in a mountain could be of help, yet with their unshakeable fortitude, the Apus held and protected me through a perilous lost night. Now, it was my heart that felt lost and abandoned on unmapped terrain. My greatest fear had been losing Jon. I didn't know what my life would look like without him. The profound and simple wisdom that reverberated in the high mountain desert rang true once again. "If you do not take fear and worry with you here, why take it with you anywhere?"

The teachings of the Apus were weaving themselves into the deepest structures of my being, occupying space that for so long had been held by beliefs of lack and limitation. They were beliefs that originated not only in the consciousness of my family but also in the consciousness of a culture that has held the patriarch in higher value and esteem through eons of time, though its threads were coming undone. What I feared most had happened: Jon left. And he had left with another woman. I was still standing. I had no idea what the steps ahead would look like, but I did know that the karmic knots of fear and worry were unraveling.

The Divine Feminine resides in mystery. She asks that we find a comfort with uncertainty. She calls on our trust, since much of the walk is unknown. The further we go on our spiritual path, the less the mind can guide us. Knowing changes from the rational to the intuitive. We can no longer rigidly hold on to beliefs and say this is for certain. We cannot take an unwavering stance and also evolve. Flexibility is needed. We must differentiate between the mind that wants to cling to something to make it so and the soul that resides in an unfolding mystery. This is the presence of the Divine Feminine rising. She needs tenderness as she ascends from darkness, no different from the sprout that is newly broken through the soil. Blow your prayers and intention into seeds to awaken the Divine Feminine within you and plant them in soil. As you nurture these seeds, you nurture the blossoming of your own divinity.

To be in light is to be enlightened. The way of light is the way of all seekers. Ironically, seeking is not the way that light can be found. We must search until the search becomes exhausted, until darkness descends. For the darkness is where light can be found. We are always looking for light, but look to darkness. It is in our darkest moment that light appears.

Enlightenment is like that.

CHAPTER TWENTY-FIVE

Hand in Hand

HOW DO WE MOVE FROM a fear-based culture to one built on love? Where is the road map? It begins within each of us. Trust is the guidepost. We must trust in the path, however much we may feel we are lost. Our destiny does not lie in the many false prophets that have led us astray, led us into the fields of failure, as a culture and as a species.

We are destined for greatness. That is why we are here. You must see yourself bigger than you have ever imagined. The world will not change with your small voice. Your highest voice, your true voice, your soul voice is what will make this happen. To change your life and rise above your wounds is an ascension. It is the journey each one of us must take. When we vision from a higher vantage point, we are visioning from the source of Creation, the womb from which we have birthed. We are visioning a world of the highest possible order of our soul.

To hold a vision is your most paramount spiritual task. A vision that is clear, that has risen above the challenges, agendas, false prophets, and sorrow is what creates a new world. A high and clear vision is needed for a new way of seeing on our planet. This is what is needed: visionaries who have risen from the weight of their wounds to create a new way of seeing the world from a higher vantage point.

The world changes when you smile at a stranger. It changes when you stop to smell a flower. It changes when you say hello to a morning bird that has come to visit. It changes because your heart changes and your heart is that powerful. You are that powerful. You are that Creator. The Creator that made our world lives in you. You are not separate from it. This is why it is important to see from the top of the mountain. From there, your vision can be clear.

Your vision is your legacy. It is your imprint. It will remain long after you are gone. Your vision lives on through time and space through your intent. Even when you no longer exist in human form, your intent lives beyond the finite existence of your body. There is no need to know how to create a new world order or when it will happen but rather know that it is time. This is what is so desperately needed now on our planet.

There are very few places where I can see the matriarch in power or point to and say this is what the Divine Feminine looks like. The most penetrating embodiment of the Divine Feminine for me took place far from home. We are often so blind to our cultural conditioning that awareness only comes to light through the lens of another culture. During the nine years I traveled to Peru, our journeys always involved a mountain trek with the shamans of the high Andes. One year, we spent an afternoon in the village of Amaru before heading into the mountains. Amaru is a traditional farming and weaving community whose people follow the ways of their ancestors. They live in harmony with our Earth Mother, Pachamama.

The small village of modest adobe homes is surrounded by lush green hills and gently sloping countryside. The women of Amaru greeted our group of twenty Western women on a bright and sunny afternoon in early May. We were showered in rose petals as we passed through the small entryway into the center of the village. We were adorned with traditional native apparel. A flat-topped black hat sat atop our heads with colored fabric draped around the brim. The hat was tied under our chins to keep it secure. Black wool textile skirts with intricately woven multi-colored bands were tucked around our waists. Our shoulders were draped in ponchos of bright geometric mosaics. The women of Amaru sang songs in Quechua, their native tongue, while we all did a circle dance. Offerings of gratitude to the Apus, to Pachamama, and to each other were made with coca leaves before heading to the fields. Our group of women was enveloped in their wholehearted welcome.

Dressed alike in native attire, we all began a gentle stroll to nearby fields to harvest quinoa and fava beans. Eagles soared overhead as we ambled through the bucolic landscape. After our previous treks in the high mountains of the Andes, the rolling hills of Amaru were an easy stroll yet the young women of the village kept running up and down our procession to help us over a little stream or guide us around a rock. We waved off their gestures with a smile.

After a short time, the women of Amaru asked our guide and interpreter, "Why don't they touch each other?" The women wondered why we kept rejecting the offer of their hands as we rambled through the countryside. In reaching out to us, they were not saying, "You look like you could use help" or "You seem a little shaky" or "I don't think you can do this on your own." Yet that was our perception of their gesture and intent. We were all so culturally conditioned to value self-reliance rather than accepting help. I can do it myself. "Thank you but no thank you" was the posture we held.

Their extension of a hand had nothing to do with the kind of thoughts we carried in our cumbersome Western egos. It was a gesture from the heart, pure and simple. Each time we waved them off, we were dismissing that connection. To the women of Amaru, we must have seemed callous, maybe even cruel, and certainly cold-hearted.

We were devastated to realize we had insulted our beautiful hosts. Once we understood their intent, our trek was thoroughly transformed. It was as if our hearts had been polished to see the purity in their gesture. From that moment on, we reached out to take a hand whenever it was extended it to us. Our journey became a divine connection of hearts, one that felt sacred. Our perspective was radically altered by the women of Amaru with their gift from a culture and language that was unknown to us. The knee jerk response we so mindlessly offered had been woven into us through a culture that valued self-reliance over connection, the individual over the group—the masculine archetype which dominated the consciousness we'd been raised in.

My first sense of what enlightenment might be envisioned the path as that of a lone traveler climbing a spiritual mountain toward Nirvana at the peak. The shift to a feminine path of Enlightenment values the journey of the whole over that of the individual. What matters is that *everyone* makes it to the mountaintop. We are not enlightened until all are enlightened. We are not free until each of us is free.

In a feminine paradigm, your hand is forever reaching—to those in front who show the way, to those behind to offer help. The Enlightenment we move toward is not as sole individuals but as a shared humanity. We are not separate from each other but inextricably woven together. Each of us matters. To understand the guidance of the divine hand is not our job. That is only a need of the mind. Our job on the path to Enlightenment is one of the heart. What that path might feel like is what the gentle women of Amaru showed us.

The profound teachings did not come from a pulpit. They were not shouted from a mountaintop.

The teachings came from women of the field.

Women whose language I did not speak.

Women whose culture I did not understand.

The most enlightened teachings of the Divine Feminine came from women who reached out their hands—as I am now reaching out mine to you. Take these stories, outstretched from my heart, as we rise together to the mountaintop where the Divine Feminine awakes and awaits us. Hand in hand.

Enlightenment is like that.

ABOUT THE AUTHOR

Karen Chrappa, a holistic physiotherapist, has served thousands of people on a healing path woven from a lifetime of dedicated studies in ancient and contemporary medicine ways. She has traveled extensively with the shamans of the Andes to Awaken the Divine Feminine. Born in New York City, she currently resides in Abiquiu where she serves the rural communities of northern New Mexico as a physical therapist.

Learn more at www.beyondfearmemoir.com

ABOUT MANGO MOON MEDIA

Mango Moon Media is a full-service social impact marketing and publishing company dedicated to empowering positive change at the intersection of business and social impact.

We publish stories and content that have the power to ignite change and make a lasting impact on society. We support authors who dare to explore the depths of human experience and present ideas that can reshape the world.

At Mango Moon Media, we embrace both innovation and tradition, offering a unique hybrid publishing model that blends the advantages of traditional publishing with the flexibility of modern methods. We are committed to supporting authors throughout their publishing journey, ensuring their creative visions shine brightly in the literary landscape. Our mission is to provide an exceptional publishing experience, where every story we share contributes to a better, more connected world.

Learn more at www.mangomoonmedia.com